To Hell with Heaven

An Introduction to Apatheism

To Hell with Heaven

An Introduction to Apatheism

Adam Kunz

HYPATIA PRESS

Copyright © 2024 Adam Kunz

All rights reserved. No part of this publication may be reproduced, stored in or introduced into a retrieval system or transmitted in any form or by any means, electronic, mechanical, photocopying, recording or otherwise without prior written permission from the publisher.

Published by Hypatia Press in the United Kingdom in 2024

ISBN: 978-1-83919-507-5

Figures 1 and 2 illustrations copyright © Adam Kunz 2024

www.hypatiapress.org

To Emily: my "light in dark places, when all other lights go out."

Contents

Preface	1
The Basics of Apatheism	15
From Intensity to Indifference	36
Reciprocity: Private and Public	70
The "Big Three" Attitudes	104
Who Cares?	148
Moving On	182

Preface

Belief, then, is a passion, the strength of which, like every other passion, is in precise proportion to the degrees of excitement.
– Percy Bysshe Shelley

As the title implies, my overarching goal in writing this book is to give an account of apatheism: what it is, why it matters, and why you (probably) are an apatheist of some variety. As I hope you will come to see, apatheism is not only a perfectly viable attitude with regard to religious claims; it is often the default position for many people, religious or not. My argument is that apatheism has many rich and rewarding facets, bringing together a collection of feelings toward religion and deity that zealots all too often dismiss as inferior or destructive. This book is meant to be an empowering account as to why those views are ill-informed, at best. Before I turn to that account, though, I feel it necessary to explain a few important points, namely: why I am writing this book, for whom I'm writing it, and the limits of what I plan to accomplish with this short volume.

First, the purpose of this book is partially intellectual and partially personal – whether those two things are even distinct in the first place. I am writing in a time period and location in which zealous religious thinking – whether tied to an organized religion or simply "religious-esque" ideology – has taken up more than its fair share of our attention in the United States. A resident of the US living in 2024 and being even marginally aware of current events would have no problem knowing what I am talking about. Religious exemptions to vaccinations, religious teaching in schools, religious-based science skepticism, religious arguments for recognizing (or not recognizing) the existence of countries, appeals to deity for identity tolerance (or intolerance) – the list could be endless. These are overtly informed by religious zeal. At the same time, political and cultural ideologies bear all the hallmarks of religious zealotry: purity tests, public sins that demand forgiveness, excommunication from social groups, and public performances that look an awful lot like rituals. These are not overtly religious, but many of the techniques and much of the rhetoric supporting them look an awful lot like religious zeal. While this is not a purely American problem, it has particular salience in the United States given the Constitution's expansive (and expanding) protections for religion and the Protestant ethic that has informed American culture from its inception.

What I find most striking about this reality is how little the average American actually participates in [insert hand waving] all of this. Login to social media or surround yourself with the constant news cycle, and you would think that the typical American has gone mad with cultish fervor. Many other authors have addressed this topic, primarily from the vantage point of belief. Those accounts focus on the role of intellectual divisions in the United States. They frame this debate as between multiple schisms: the Evangelical Christians, the atheists, the mainstream Protestants, Catholics, etc. For example, when I began this book in 2020, the country was engaged in a large debate over COVID-19 vaccination exemptions or mandatory shutdowns of public events, including religious services. Commentators considered these debates in the context of the type of faith (or lack thereof) at issue, the sect promoting it, and the doctrinal reasons motivating their willingness to comply with state action. This belief-oriented framework is, of course, helpful; it gives us a sense for how beliefs relate to one another and how they have direct impact on actions. I am in no way disparaging that framework.

But what I wish to do in this book is approach the religious schisms in a civil society from a different viewpoint: attitude. As I explain in Chapter 1, religious attitude is the amount of emotional and psychological energy we dedicate to our beliefs. While there is considerable overlap between belief and attitude, I believe the latter is ultimately what is shaping much of our discourse and the presentation of it in the media. Attitudes – or rather the attitudes of a shrill minority – are vastly more important to me at the moment than the beliefs that inform them. Just being a Christian or an atheist cannot capture the full reality of a person's actions; their attitudes are just as much in the driver's seat. My hope is that this book will encourage us to reframe our accounts of religious differences to unpack their nuances – rather than fit them neatly into ideological buckets.

Now, to the personal. This book is the outgrowth of almost four decades of living the full range of attitudes that I describe in the following chapters. To put my cards on the table: I am a former member of The Church of Jesus Christ of Latter-day Saints – aka, a Mormon. I grew up in a small town in Idaho founded by my Mormon ancestors who left their homes in Europe in the late-1800s with the hope that they were living in the "end of days" and would prepare to meet their god (as soon as possible) in the Great Basin of the Rocky Mountains. I lived among Mormons for the first 25 years of my life. I have hundreds of family members and friends who are or were raised Mormon. I was taught by Mormons. I attended a Mormon church every Sunday that I can remember – three hours, each week, at the time. I attended a Mormon seminary during high school. I left home at age 19 and served a two-year Mormon mission, which, at that time, required little-to-no contact with my family, a rigid schedule, daily proselytizing, and a near-poverty lifestyle – a privilege, I might add, for which my parents and I paid tens of thousands of dollars. I married a Mormon woman when I was age 22 in a Mormon temple. I attended a Mormon institute of religion during my time as an undergraduate at a Mormon university. I wrote papers, read books, and talked with scholars on Mormonism. I presented at Mormon symposia. Throughout my time in law school and as a practicing attorney in Washington, DC, I volunteered my time weekly at a Mormon temple and officiated the most sacred and secretive Mormon religious ceremonies. I actively served in positions of leadership and teaching in my Mormon communities. I gave 10 percent of my income to the Mormon Church starting with the very first dollar I ever earned. I fasted, prayed, volunteered, and gave nearly three decades of my life to Mormonism. I lived nearly the first three decades of my life deep in the Mormon religion.

Beyond these hallmarks of belief, though, my attitude was very much of Mormon zealotry. I filtered every topic through the lens of Mormonism. Although I was raised in a comparatively, politically liberal home, I nevertheless explained those views on the basis of Mormon doctrine. Choices like what food or drinks to consume, what clothes to wear, what types of women I should date, the things I should study in school, and the kind of profession I should choose were all based around Mormon doctrine. When I debated people on topics like politics, culture, and philosophy, I constantly framed it through my Mormon beliefs. I also greatly desired that other people would be Mormon – I strongly believed that the world would be better off if we were all Mormon. I viewed major catastrophes in the world during my adolescence and young adulthood as events that proved the Mormon account of the world ending – Y2K, 9/11, climate change, earthquakes and tsunamis, wildfires, hurricanes, economic instability, war. When I lost a loved one, it was because the Mormon deity had a purpose in taking them, but I was assured that we would see each other again in the afterlife. And I believed that someday – likely and hopefully very, very soon – Jesus would return to Earth by coming to the United States, setting up a utopian society called Zion with Mormonism as its foundation, ruling over the earth from the United States, and preparing the world for final judgement according to Mormon doctrine. If I was not a Mormon zealot, then I challenge anyone to explain to me what I was.

And then one day, time and space broke open. It started as a small crack in my psyche but grew bigger and bigger until one day it engulfed my whole worldview. Quit unexpectedly and without my wanting it to, everything I had been taught and had believed from infancy began to melt away, leaving me naked and alone in a cold, black universe, unmoored and desperate for any beliefs to which I could cling. The full story of that journey is for another time and another context, but suffice to say that, over the course of many tear-filled years, I unlearned my zeal. People who leave dogmatic faiths describe the process as "deprogramming," but that does not fully capture the experience and underplays the raw emotions at work. A better term would be "psychological rebirth": painful, lengthy, and lonely labor and delivery of a new mentality. Today, I stand on the backside of that journey, calm and resolute in my new worldview, confident in who I have become, and empathetic for those who have gone or will go through similar experiences.

Why? Because I simply no longer care. At least, not about all of the many, many metaphysical and cosmic things that I was taught or believed I was supposed to care about. Make no mistake: I care deeply about the journey of one's faith, about topics like death and consciousness, about morality and humanity, and about a building a better world. But whether I am or am not pleasing a god is no longer a question to which I give much thought. Whether that being exists is an unimportant question to me. Whether that being looks and acts like humans, is a pantheon of persons, is a spiritual presence, or is an unfeeling amorphous blob from a H.P. Lovecraft short story – these things no longer bother me. Whether I will or will not stand before that being to be judged is an irrelevant question to my existence. Do I have some beliefs about those questions, or have I formed preliminary answers to them? Yes. I am some form of strong agnostic that tends toward soft atheism. But those beliefs are so far in the backseat of my life that they are in the trunk. What really, truly informs my life now – the attitude with which I face those questions and many related ones – is an active, committed indifference.

For that reason, I have paired the philosophical work in this book with autobiographical examples, making this book partially my own story and partially a book of theory. I am an apatheist. I have become an apatheist after having been a committed zealot. At the same time, I am a political theorist and constitutional law scholar that studies religious freedom in the United States. For that reason, it is very hard for me to separate my own story from the views I have on religious attitudes. The thoughts I share in this book are, then, personal and professional. If autobiography is a difficult genre for you or you find it an unpersuasive source of truth, you may find this book hard to digest. But as I hope you will come to see if you follow my thought process, the term "apatheism" contains more power than it seems at first blush. My story is meant to convey how that concept has real, life-changing meaning. And, I strongly believe, that if you have picked up a copy of this book, you will see parts of yourself in it.

That brings me to the intended audience for this book. I have in mind someone like me, who already feels apatheistic attitudes and who already has a sense for how it feels to live by that attitude. You may have already heard the term and may have even begun to use it, but my suspicion is that you do not yet have a framework for articulating it. If you were to sit down and work through the logic of your position, you would likely be able to develop some talking points for those who ask you what your attitude toward religion is. But you might not have the time, resources, or energy to do so. This book is written for you. My hope is that by the time you have finished reading, you will have a clear account of what apatheism is, how it is distinguished from zeal, what kinds of topics it is directed to, and how you can talk about it to others. For you, this book should be an affirmation of your intuitions.

That means that some readers will likely find this book deficient. The ardent zealot will most likely gain very little from my discussion in the next several chapters; in fact, I expect that many religious zealots will be very angry at my account. Likewise, those who come to apatheism from a point of skepticism will likely still remain skeptical once they have set down this book. The reason for that is not because these readers are not open to learning about a new subject or are incapable of understanding. Rather, it is because *I am not trying to convince either the zealot or the skeptic.* This book is descriptive – it explains a phenomenon and provides scaffolding for further discussion. It is not normative – at no point will I argue that anyone *should* be an apatheist or that apatheism is *preferable* to zeal. Nor do I provide a handbook or set of instructions for living as an apatheist. Rest assured, I am working on those topics in separate projects; I do strongly believe that more people should be apatheists and that there are steps one can take to live an apatheistic life. But I am choosing to set those topics to the side for now and concentrate on understanding apatheism first. Because this topic has received very little attention in public discourse, I feel it deserves a fair shot at being taken seriously. As I constantly remind my students, intellectual humility is a key requirement of learning: you must understand something before you can debate and critique it. If you have picked up this book to be convinced, I would ask that you pump the brakes for the moment and first try to understand what some of your fellow humans feel toward religion. We can take up the normative and practical questions later.

Finally, that brings me to the limits and scope of what I am doing in this book. In order to provide a clear picture of what apatheism is, I have broken down the topic into constituent parts. Because I am first and foremost a political theorist, my end goal is to understand apatheism as a public phenomenon, especially as to how different citizens interact with one another. But in order to arrive at that point, I first need to lay significant groundwork. For that reason, I begin in Chapter 1 with an orientation of the basics of apatheism: a proposed definition, the factors one would consider in being an apatheist, and the general terminology that an apatheist would use to discuss it with others.

In the subsequent chapters, I build upon this introduction. In Chapter 2, I start the hard work of distinguishing between apatheism and its attitudinal opposite – zealotry. In that chapter, I explain that the difference between the two is one of degree of feeling: zealots have intense attitudes to their religious beliefs, while apatheists are indifferent or passive. I continue distinguishing these attitudes in Chapter 3, where I explore the exceptionalism that's at the heart of zealotry and the commitment to religious reciprocity that makes apatheism different. In doing so, I also describe how apatheism can have both a private and a public component – apatheism for individual life and apatheism for public life. In Chapter 4, I dive deeper into the various ways that an apatheist might express themselves. I believe there are at least three different subsidiary claims about deities that an apatheist might be indifferent to, and I show what each of them looks like. All of these chapters are the philosophical foundation for apatheism.

I close out the book in Chapter 5 by discussing why apatheism matters, why it serves as a moderating force, and why we should be talking more about it. I have as a future goal to write a full book on the value of apatheism (why one *should* be an apatheist), but for now, this chapter opens a window into why we should even care about apatheism. Finally, I conclude by tying my discussion back to my original purpose. Additionally, I preview where I plan to go in the future.

All of this means that I have necessarily had to be selective in what I discuss. This is a short book and only a sketch of apatheism. For a concept that has received little attention, I think we have to start somewhere. It is not a philosophical treatise, and the average academic would likely have much to say about this book at a conference. This book is not intended for peer review, it does not cite an expansive literary background on the subject, and it does not comment endlessly on previous writers. Additionally, zealots will call foul on much of what I have provided here. I know this and acknowledge both realities; I do not, then, take it as valid criticism of this book that I have not done and said everything about the topic. Moreover, I acknowledge that I am an imperfect speaker: I have lived the life of a zealot and an apatheist, so my experience may be biased.

That said, I am offering everything in this book as a way to begin a conversation. This is not the end of a dialogue but an invitation to begin one. Insofar as I have misstated or committed any fallacies, I will of course recognize them and make corrections. Nevertheless, because this book is written by an apatheist for apatheists about apatheism, I believe I am entitled to some intellectually humble freedom to converse. To put it in 2023 terms: I am hoping that some readers of this book will "feel seen." If I can do just that, I have accomplished the immediate goal and will take up harder questions later.

***

Before I begin, I also want to make two more points, both of which are about language and neither of which I hope will be controversial to most readers. The first is that I try to use "they/them/their" pronouns when referring to a hypothetical person. I find the use of the word "one" or "he or she" to be clunky and too formal. For example, consider the following sentence: "An apatheist person is one who has *their* own religious beliefs, while feeling generally indifferent to the priority of those feelings in *their* own life." I could use other pronouns in that sentence, but using the plural pronoun is becoming an increasingly effective way to communicate. I am *not* using these pronouns because of some political or cultural statement; it has nothing to do with gender identity nor am I suggesting that everyone should adopt these as their pronouns. I use these pronouns throughout the book for efficiency purposes only.

Second, as I have indicated, I will draw heavily from my personal experience in explaining what apatheism is. That requires that I refer to my own prior faith and religious beliefs. In doing so, I will, as I have already done, use the word "Mormon" to refer to a member of The Church of Jesus Christ of Latter-day Saints, the phrase "Mormon church" to refer to the organization headquartered in Salt Lake City, Utah, and the word "Mormonism" to refer to the doctrines and beliefs of Mormons and the Mormon church. I recognize that, as of this writing, this church and its members consider the usage of the word "Mormon" to be offensive – in some cases, going as far as to call the word a "religious slur."

Nevertheless, I will use this word for a few reasons. For one, the word is more efficient and recognizable by a non-Mormon audience than the mouthful "member of The Church of Jesus Christ of Latter-day Saints" or "Latter-day Saint." Why say in ten words what can be said in one? Additionally, the word Mormon has been used for hundreds of years by members and non-members alike – overwhelmingly to the benefit of the church. For example, less than two decades ago, the Mormon church used the phrase in advertising campaigns and news releases. Social media users would have seen the church's multi-billion dollar "I am a Mormon" campaign that ran from 2010 to 2018 in which individual believers were depicted in short videos proudly declaring that they are Mormons.[1] The linguistic change in August 2018 was prompted by the new presidency of Russell Nelson, then the most senior apostle. Nelson had been decrying the usage of the word since the 1990s,[2] but it was only after gaining the absolute and unquestioned authority of prophet that Nelson could mandate the change within the church and demand it from the public. Nelson's only explanation was that his god told him to make the change.[3] At the same time, the Mormon church retains a trademark on the term and has threatened lawsuits against those it believes have appropriated it.[4] When we talk of an unchanging god, you have to wonder about why such a god was fine with a word for so long, abruptly switched course when his spokesperson changed, and vehemently fights to protect the word while it discourages its use. My own prophecy, from my 30 plus years in the Mormon church, is that it will come back into vogue again when the leadership inevitably changes hands once again.

But putting those reasons aside, I use this word for a very important reason: to reclaim it for those of us who have distanced themselves from the church. As the church has demanded a language shift and many in the media have acquiesced to that demand on ill-informed, culturally relative "religious freedom"

---

[1] Goodstein, Laurie. "Mormons' Ad Campaign May Play Out on the '12 Campaign Trail, *The New York Times* (Nov. 17, 2011).
[2] Nelson, Russell M. "Thus Shall My Church Be Called," *Annual General Conference* (April 1990).
[3] Julia Jacobs, "Stop Saying 'Mormon,' Church Leader Says. But Is the Real Name Too Long?," *The New York Times*, August 18, 2018, https://www.nytimes.com/2018/08/18/us/mormon-latter-day-saints-name.html.
[4] Pierce, Scott D. "Is the LDS Church suing a 'Real Housewife of SLC' over her book, 'Bad Mormon'?," *The Salt Lake Tribune* (February 1, 2023).

grounds, the voices of many former Mormons have become lost in the discussion. This small example of language is a perfect microcosm of the larger problem I discuss in this book – namely, that too often the zealots get to set the boundaries for what counts as tolerance and civil liberties at the expense of those of us who simply do not care. Whether it is requiring the word "god" to be capitalized or demanding that some individual be referred to by a title that would only be considered sacred by the believer, these zealous language games encourage a presumption that active believers get special treatment to the exclusion of the rest of us who have distanced themselves from faith.

In personal terms, I have decided to reject this language game. I do so because I want to pay respect to the 30 plus years of time, energy, and mental health that I sacrificed to the Mormon church. To put it in clear terms, it's just as offensive to me, a former Mormon, to be gaslit into thinking that a word that was good *then* but bad *now* simply because one man in Salt Lake City says he heard a voice in his head. And just as a Mormon demands their space to say what they wish about themselves, I demand the right to use the language I wish to use to convey my own ideas. This respect cuts both ways.

The Basics of Apatheism

Nothing is so fatal to religion as indifference.
– Edmund Burke

1. God Will Provide Himself a Lamb

Matthew Taylor Coleman was a surfing instructor in Santa Barbara, California, in the summer of 2021. He and his wife, Abby Droogsma Coleman, had been married since January 8, 2017, and were small businessowners, running a surfing instruction company, Lovewater Surf School.[5] As of 2021, they had been married for about three years and had two children: Kaleo and Roxy, ages two and 10-months, respectively. The Colemans were churchgoing, evangelical Christians. Matthew had attended an evangelical college in San Diego and had been a missionary in Spain and Mexico. He and Abby had met through a church group when Matthew was in his later 30s. He was active in his community as a local philanthropist and Spanish tutor. He'd spent years in community non-profits, at one point using his experience as a surf instructor to mentor local youth. Members of his community say that Matthew was the type of person who would comfort

---

[5] Lovewater Surf School, accessed November 15, 2021, https://lovewater-surf.com.

those in need – a kindhearted, civically minded individual. A childhood friend recounted that Matthew "was popular, but he didn't act like it…he was humble." By every account from the people who knew him, Matthew was an average evangelical living an unassuming, middle-class lifestyle in an unassuming corner of unassuming suburban America.

But on August 9, 2021, that façade came crashing down. As of this writing, the events of that day are still allegations and will be pieced together over the coming months and years. What is known is this: Roxy and Kaleo were brutally killed near Rosarito, Mexico – over 250 miles from their home. And Matthew has confessed to being their killer. According to FBI investigators and an affidavit in support of the indictment against Matthew, he and his family were preparing for a camping trip the previous Saturday, August 7, 2021. Abby stated that they were packing up the family van, when Matthew left with Roxy and Kaleo, leaving Abby wondering where they were going. Matthew did not respond to text messages from Abby after his initial disappearance, but the iPhone Matthew used pinpointed him in Rosarito throughout the following two days. Surveillance videos from a hotel in the area show Matthew and the children checking in on Saturday and leaving before dawn on Monday. Witnesses at the hotel said that Matthew returned a few hours later, alone, and checked out.

Abby had contacted Santa Barbara Police on Saturday and filed a missing person report on Sunday. When Matthew attempted to reenter the United States at San Ysidro Port of Entry, an FBI agent detained and interviewed him. The children were nowhere to be seen and blood was found on the vehicle's registration documents. Meanwhile, Roberto Salinas Ramira, a farm worker on the Rancho Del Descanso property, near Rosarito, had found the bodies of the two children. Blood splatter near his home led him to the bodies in a nearby ditch. When Mexican authorities arrived, they found large puncture wounds in their chest cavities.

Matthew was interviewed by the FBI and confessed to killing his children. He identified the bodies as those of his children, and he told investigators where to find his discarded bloody clothes along with the murder weapon – a spearfishing gun he owned. According to investigators, Matthew said he had taken Roxy and Kaleo across the U.S./Mexico border that weekend with the intent to kill them. He left so quickly that the van was not equipped with a car seat for 10-month-old Roxy, so he had placed her in a box for the more than four-hour journey. He also described in detail how he had led the children on to the remote property on the morning of August 9th, carrying the spearfishing gun with him. He said he then shot Roxy in the chest and described how he had aimed for her heart. He attempted to do the same to two-year-old Kaleo, but when the toddler did not die immediately, Matthew described that he moved the spear around. He stated that he left the property, discarded the spearfishing gun in a creek, and returned to the hotel. On his way through Tijuana toward the border, he discarded his clothing in a trash can off the side of the road.

If these abhorrent facts are true, the Coleman children's murders are shocking in themselves. As a father of a son who is only slightly older than Kaleo, I have no frame of reference for what Matthew says he did to his children, nor do you. Put yourself in the shoes of every participant in this alleged drama. Picture the initial excitement of Kaleo as his father loaded up him and his baby sister for a planned camping trip. The mix of confusion and trust at not knowing why mom wasn't in her usual spot in the van. The novelty of checking into a hotel and spending Saturday night and all of Sunday with Dad – a whole day alone with him! The thrill of waking up early in the morning on Monday, driving out to a new place…maybe this was the camping spot. And then picture the fear and confusion that crossed Kaleo's face as dad plunged a spear through his baby sister's body. What were Kaelo's thoughts? What did Kaleo try to do in those final moments, when one of two people he trusted most did something so unspeakable? What were his thoughts when the gun was turned on him, writhing in pain as Dad moved the spear around his chest, his last image being the face of a man who had been there from the moment he was born.

Now put yourself in Abby's shoes, 250 miles away. Imagine her confusion when her husband drove off with their children. Think of the initial rationalizations. Maybe he was running an errand before the camping trip or checking in with work. A few text messages to him go unanswered. Soon the confusion turns to anger – he's driven off without Roxy's car seat, the trip is moments away, why hasn't he responded? Then the anger turns to fear. His iPhone shows him driving south to Mexico, and by that evening, he is in some far-flung part of Baja. She has no reason yet to doubt her children's safety – he's their father, they're in good hands. He just needs to come back now. She calls the police. Saturday turns to Sunday, and he still hasn't responded. The police need a missing persons report to track him down. Yes, they're missing. Yes, let's bring them home. Monday morning, and still no responses from him, but his iPhone shows he's driving north. Thank god! He's coming back. And then the call comes in from the police. They've detained Matthew. He says he's done something unthinkable. She comes down to the station and is told that her children are dead, brutally killed, and the man who's confessed is their father – the man who's loved and held and cared for and nurtured this family from the beginning. Imagine the waves of disbelief, denial, anger, crippling grief, and shocked dismay washing over Abby. The last image of her family as she had come to know was of happy children and a loving husband.

Now last of all, try – even if it's rightly difficult to do so – to put yourself in Matthew's shoes. What could have led him to whisk away his children away from Abby like that? What thoughts were in his head as he placed his infant daughter in a box and put her and her toddler brother in the van? How long had he been planning this, their last father-child outing? As he careened down the freeway toward Mexico, what did he tell them? What did he tell himself? In the two final nights he stayed with his children in a hotel room, did he have any doubts? And that Monday morning, did he resolve himself? Did he walk confidently with his children to the van, drive to a remote property, and walk with his children into a patch of ground nearby? Was he even aware of his surroundings or had his mind become so warped that nothing around him mattered any longer? Did he hesitate at all before pulling the trigger – not once, but twice? What went through his head as he watched his children bleed out in front of him? Did he feel anything at all when he heard their final cries and watched their faces twist in agony and betrayal? And what did he think as he drove away? What was he going to do now? What was he going to say to everyone in the neighborhood? What would he tell his family? What would he tell Abby?

2. From Belief to Zeal

I apologize for the brutality of this story, but I share it with a purpose. If the events Matthew described are true, then this is one of those rare, gruesome filicides that we would hear or read about, look at in disgust, and move on with hope that the survivors can find some kind of healing. Tragedies involving children, including murders, happen every day in every country in the world. Why would I bother to share this one, especially in a book about apatheism? Because in addition to confessing to the murders, Matthew told investigators why he had committed them. Matthew said, according to the investigator's affidavit, that "he believed his children were going to grow into monsters so he had to kill them." Matthew had been receiving visions and signs that Abby possessed serpent DNA and that this DNA had been passed along to his children. From Matthew's perspective, his actions were not horrific, but heroic. He had to do what he did to "save[] the world from monsters."[6]

Matthew got these ideas from QAnon, a community of conspiracy theorists that originated in October 2017 through the internet forum 4chan. An anonymous user calling themselves "Q" claimed to be a high-level government employee with the U.S. Department of Energy under the administration of Donald Trump. Q claimed to have access to Top Secret-level government information that revealed the "truth" behind the investigation of Trump by special prosecutor, Robert Mueller. While the rest of the public believed that the Mueller investigation's mission was to pursue claims of Russian interference in the 2016 Presidential Election, Q claimed that this was all a façade. Rather, the Mueller investigation was really intended to uncover criminal activity of former President Barack Obama, the 2016 Democratic nominee, Hilary Clinton, and other high-ranking liberals. The alleged crimes? Kidnapping children, torturing and sexually abusing them, using them in satanic rituals, and draining their bodies of adrenochrome to be used in drugs.

Although the group itself is by no means a religion, its ties to evangelical and extremist Christianity have been well documented.

---

[6] For more on the Coleman children murders, see Kevin T. Dugan, "QAnon's Deadly Price," *RolingStone* online, October 9, 2021, https://www.rollingstone.com/culture/culture-features/matthew-taylor-coleman-qanon-children-killing-1239151/; Neil Vigdor, " Surf Instructor Killed His Children and Claimed QAnon Made Him Do It, F.B.I. Says," *The New York Times* online, August 12, 2021, https://www.nytimes.com/2021/08/12/us/matthew-coleman-children-mexico.html; "Man says he killed his kids over QAnon conspiracy theories," *CBS News* online, August 12, 2021, https://www.cbsnews.com/news/matthew-taylor-coleman-qanon-kill-kids-california-serpent-dna-conspiracy/.

The group often uses Christian imagery and rhetoric to spread its message: end-times eschatology, the rise of an Anti-Christ, evil cabals manipulating the word order, and prophetic utterances that only believers can hear. Trump serves as the object of salvation for adherents, a prophetic figure who will use the power of the U.S. government to thwart the Anti-Christ. At the furthest fringe of the movement, one QAnon group claimed that President John F. Kennedy or his son, John Jr., (or both) would be resurrected or return from hiding to join in the fight; this particular group is led by a man named Michael Brian Protzman, who claims to be a representative of the Christian god. The number of enemies these people have identified is vast, including non-political figures like Tom Hanks and Chrissy Teigen, and even figures who are otherwise politically aligned with the group, like President Trump's former National Security Advisor, Michael Flynn. At the bare minimum, the group has framed itself as god-fearing believers fighting against a cult that follows the Christian version of the devil – a cosmic fight between good and evil.[7] Moreover, while the shadowy figure Q is not a religious figure, nor is the group organized as an institute of religion, Christians are overwhelmingly represented in the group. Evangelicals, non-

---

[7] The coverage on QAnon from inception until this writing is extensive. For light reading on it, I recommend "America's Satanic Panic Returns – This Time Through QAnon," NPR online, May 18, 2021,
https://www.npr.org/2021/05/18/997559036/americas-satanic-panic-returns-this-time-through-qanon; Justin Caffier, "A Guide to QAnon, the New King of Right-Wing Conspiracy Theories," Vice online, June 12, 2018, https://www.vice.com/en/article/ywex8v/what-is-qanon-conspiracy-theory. For more in-depth reading, see Mike Rothschild. *The Storm Is Upon Us*, (Brooklyn, NY: Melville House Publishing, May 2021).

denominational, and unaffiliated Christians make up the largest populations.

Social media posts and statements by people who know him point to the fact that Matthew Coleman was heavily influenced by this online community. In the midst of the pandemic, Matthew feared the end of the world was coming and that believers like him were seeing the "signs of the end times" in Q's warnings. The fear of a devil-worshipping cult secretly controlling everything is a political trope that has played out repeatedly in American history, often coinciding with changes in electoral politics; its most recent iteration was the "Satanic panic" of the 1970s and 1980s, coinciding with the rise of Regan conservatism. Trying to parse out what is religion and what is politics in Matthew's actions, then, is likely unhelpful, as he, like many other QAnon adherents, do not see much of a distinction between the two concepts – politics is an expression of belief and belief makes politics salient.[8]

Aside from his ties to QAnon, Matthew's admitted reasons for killing Roxy and Kaleo bear an eerie resemblance to the biblical foundations of Christianity, and its cousins, Judaism and Islam. Recall the story of Abraham, the father of monotheistic faith and the archetype of the righteous believer in god. Abraham hears god's voice speaking to him and sees visions of a promise that god makes to him: a multitude of heirs that will be as numberless as

---

[8] To review these data, see the January 2020 American Perspectives Survey by the Survey Center on American Life and Paul A. Djupe and Ryan P. Burge, "A Conspiracy at the Heart of It: Religion and Q," *Religion in Public* online, November 6, 2020, https://religioninpublic.blog/2020/11/06/a-conspiracy-at-the-heart-of-it-religion-and-q/.

the sands of the sea. To Iron Age Abraham, this is no less than the promise of immortality. All Abraham must do, so the voice tells him, is covenant with god to do his divine will. It is not until much later that he and his wife, Sarah, produce and heir, Isma'il or Ishaq (depending on which version of events you accept). After a time, that same voice of god commands Abraham to take a three-day journey with his son into the wilderness, ascend Mount Moriah, and offer up his child as a burnt sacrifice to god.

Abraham follows these instructions down to the letter, to the point that he laid his son on the altar and prepared to drive a knife into him, only to be stopped at the last minute by the voice. In exchange for this show of piety, god promises Abraham that the covenant is fulfilled. The traditional versions of Judaic and Islamic doctrine teach that this Abrahamic moment serves as the basis for their religious existence, while Christian tradition sees the story as a foreshadowing of Jesus's crucifixion. The overlaps with Matthew's story are striking: the voices and visions, parent-child relationship, the long journey into the wilderness, a commitment to sacrificing a child for a higher purpose. The only differences are of time period and end result. Unfortunately, there was no voice that stayed Matthew's hand.

I have chosen Matthew's story, but I could have chosen many other acts of religious zeal that led to death and destruction. There are the obvious historical examples: the Christian Crusades in the medieval period, the sacking of Constantinople, the expansion of Muslim empires preceding the Ottoman empire, the religious wars in Europe, any number of Zionist conflicts. It also is not worth recounting the many acts of terrorism that have been committed throughout the world in the 20th and 21st Centuries in the name of religion or religious persecution.

But beyond those geopolitical instances, there are the more personal, recent ones similar to Matthew's: the killings of his two daughters by Yaser Abdel Said in Texas in 2008 for dating Christian men; the killing of abortion physician George Tiller in Kansas by fundamentalist Scott Roeder in 2009; the Christian-motivated attack on a Jewish synagogue by John Earnest in 2019; the allegedly religious-motivated murder of a Muslim family of four by Christian extremist Nathaniel Veltman in Ontario in 2021. It is far beyond the scope of this book to recount every instance of cruelty done out of zealous belief; the Coleman children's murder just happens to be the most salient and most recent as of this writing. But I want to use this story as an entry point for what apatheism is and why it matters. As I will explain, apatheism stands in stark contrast to the kind of attitude that Matthew or any other zealot embraces, and I believe many of us already display it.

Before I proceed, I want to make two things very clear about Matthew's story. First and foremost, it should go without saying that no sane person would make such statements and take such actions that Matthew made that August day in 2021. Matthew almost certainly has some form of mental illness, the severity of which and whether he was seeking treatment for it remains to be seen. In a larger sense, it's hard to imagine a father turning a weapon on his children without having some form of mental instability. Indeed, in October 2023, a federal judge deemed Matthew incompetent to stand trial and ordered him to be committed for treatment. As of this writing, the court will not revisit that decision until March 2024.

So, I am in no way disregarding how much mental health played a role in Roxy's and Kaleo's deaths. But as the stigma of mental illness has dissipated over the last several decades, there is a growing awareness that many people throughout the developed world are dealing with some form of mental instability – and the vast majority of them are not taking a spearfishing gun to their children. Mental illness might have been a factor, but it certainly was not the only one. For that matter, what separates Matthew's mental state from that of any zealous adherent to a belief? Any act of violence done in the name of zealotry would likely have some form of mental illness at its base, as one would need a high level of obsession to do the sorts of things that zealots do. History is rife with examples of "heroes" who defended their ideas to the point of bloodshed; that we happen to be on the outside looking in with regard to Matthew's ideas should not make us so quick to dismiss this as just another example of "someone going off the rails." Judged in that light, the Spanish Inquisition or the witch hunts of Salem could be just as easily dismissed as aberrations, unworthy of analysis. What's more, if the "divine" voice in Matthew's head had told him to instead take his children for a day trip to Disneyland, would that have prompted opinions about his mental competence?

Second, I am not so arrogant in my own views to suggest that religion is a sufficient condition for cruelty. Just as every mentally ill person is not out there killing their children, neither is every religious person. Not every Christian bursts into a synagogue bent on murdering Jews out of some deluded vengeance for the Crucifixion. Not every Muslim flies planes into office buildings. Not every evangelical who believes the fatuous ramblings of an online troll is planning to turn on their family. Religious belief alone is not the fuel that brings a person to commit heinous acts that they otherwise would not. This book is not an indictment against religious belief.

However, I cite the example of Matthew Coleman because it displays something that I think many people, religious or otherwise, sense when they hear stories like his. The murder of the Coleman children presents us as viewers with a puzzle: what made an otherwise normal, average evangelical Christian who happened to espouse conspiratorial views do something so brutal to two innocent children? The answer, I believe, lies not in belief but zeal. Matthew Coleman's knowledge claims about deity and the world are shared by millions. But the level to which he cared about those beliefs – the energy with which he committed to them – drove him to commit one of the worst acts a human can do.

3. The Public Problem

At exactly the same time as extremist groups like QAnon provide the motivating zeal for crimes like the Coleman murders, the legal landscape has given such groups constitutional cover. Even a cursory glance at recent developments should be enough to reveal the problem. In 2019, in the case of *Espinoza v. Montana Department of Revenue*,[9] the Supreme Court extended Free Exercise

---

[9] *Espinoza v. Montana Dep't of Revenue*, 140 S. Ct. 2246 (2020).

jurisprudence in a manner that should be troubling to religious moderates and secularists alike. As has been covered extensively,[10] the facts of the case are fairly straightforward. Montana had a state constitutional provision that banned public funds to schools "controlled in whole or in part by any church, sect, or denomination." This provision is called a Blaine Amendment, a tool with a long history of controversy[11] beyond the scope of this book to recount. At the same time, Montana had a tax credit program that gave favorable treatment to organizations that award scholarships to private schools. Following the Montana state constitution, the Montana Department of Revenue promulgated a rule that prevented such scholarships from being used at religious schools. The Court concluded that this violated the Free Exercise rights of families that would have otherwise used the scholarships for instruction at religious schools.

Chief Justice Roberts, writing for a conservative majority, held that, despite recent historical trends away from public support of

---

[10] Amy Howe, "Opinion analysis: Court rules that religious schools cannot be excluded from state funding for private schools," *SCOTUSblog* online, June 30, 2020, https://www.scotusblog.com/2020/06/opinion-analysis-court-rules-that-religious-schools-cannot-be-excluded-from-state-funding-for-private-schools/; Adam Liptak, "Supreme court gives religious schools more access to state aid," *The New York Times*, June 30, 2020, https://www.nytimes.com/2020/06/30/us/supreme-court-religious-schools-aid.html; Robert Barnes, "Supreme Court says states that subsidize private education must include religious schools," *The Washington Post*, June 30, 2020, https://www.washingtonpost.com/politics/courts_law/supreme-court-says-montana-program-aiding-private-schools-must-be-open-to-religious-schools/2020/06/30/4d0af7e6-bad7-11ea-bdaf-a129f921026f_story.html.

[11] Jane G. Rainey, "Blaine Amendments," *The First Amendment Encyclopedia*, https://www.mtsu.edu/first-amendment/article/1036/blaine-amendments.

religious institutions, a state cannot withhold aid simply because of religious status. Could the scholarship be used for expressly religious training (e.g., training to enter the clergy)? Maybe not. But the fact that it was left up to the individual students and their families to use the scholarships and that the schools themselves were not expressly indoctrinating students was enough to raise Free Exercise problems.

This case is sandwiched between two other cases: *Trinity Lutheran*, decided in 2016,[12] and *Fulton*, decided in 2021.[13] Like *Espinoza*, these cases involve withholding public support by a state or municipality to a religious organization. In *Trinity Lutheran*, the denied benefit was a public grant for installing playground equipment at a religious preschool and daycare. In *Fulton*, it was adoption referrals to Catholic Social Services that refused to place children with same sex foster parents. Despite the obvious tensions with the Establishment Clause's prevention of respect for a religious establishment, the justices seemed to think in *Trinity Lutheran* and *Espinoza* that public support for religion is perfectly justified – despite a democratic signal from citizens to the contrary. The Court only further extended that line of thinking in *Fulton*.

Now, contrast this line of cases with two other realities. First, consider the fact that the religious liberty in question is one rooted in a Judeo-Christian perspective. Almost reflexively, the Court will permit Free Exercise protections for Christian belief at the expense of the rights of others. Recent cases highlight this truth:

---

[12] Trinity Lutheran Church of Columbia, Inc. v. Comer, 137 S. Ct. 2012 (2017).
[13] Fulton v. City of Philadelphia, Pennsylvania, 141 S. Ct. 1868 (2021).

the right of Christian fundamentalist business owners to deny services to those who identify as queer,[14] the right of Christian fundamentalist businesses to withhold public benefits because doing so would conflict with extremist Christian doctrine,[15] and the denial of the right of taxpayers to challenge federal funding decisions that favor religious organizations.[16]

And these are just the most recent ones. In all of these cases, the Supreme Court continues to indicate that it will side with the rights of Judeo-Christian religions over those of other individuals, interest groups, and states. Meanwhile, the Court rarely does likewise with minority religions, such as Native American faiths. It has denied Free Exercise protection when the federal government, even over its own impact reports, decimates a Native American sacred site, thereby ending a faith.[17] It has carved out whole Free Exercise exceptions for "generally applicable laws" when Native American religious activities run afoul of drug laws.[18] And lower courts have routinely followed the Court's lead on these types of cases. These inconsistencies should at least give an outside viewer some pause.[19]

---

[14] Masterpiece Cakeshop, Ltd. v. Colorado C.R. Comm'n, 138 S. Ct. 1719 (2018).
[15] Burwell v. Hobby Lobby Stores, Inc., 573 U.S. 682 (2014).
[16] Hein v. Freedom From Religion Found., Inc., 551 U.S. 587 (2007).
[17] Lyng v. Nw. Indian Cemetery Protective Ass'n, 485 U.S. 439 (1988).
[18] Emp. Div., Dep't of Hum. Res. of Oregon v. Smith, 494 U.S. 872 (1990).
[19] Melemaikalani Moniz, "Treading on Sacred Ground," Freedom Forum Institute, Sept. 6, 2017,
https://www.freedomforuminstitute.org/first-amendment-center/topics/freedom-of-religion/free-exercise-clause-overview/treading-on-sacred-ground-are-native-american-sacred-sites-protected-by-the-freedom-of-religion/#_Toc492490193.

The latest round of religion cases comes at a time of increasing secularization. As of 2019, over a quarter of the United States' population no longer identifies with any religion – a number that has nearly doubled in the last 15 years. At the same time, Christianity, the United States' historically dominant faith, continues to bleed adherents at an even more rapid rate.[20] This phenomenon follows a similar trajectory in Western Europe.[21] While some continue to debate whether these statistics indicate growing secularization,[22] there is a sense among many social commentators that this trend will continue – along with a growing partisan clash over matters of faith in the public sphere.[23] To put this in the context of the recent religion cases: as more of the population moves toward a public sphere free from religion, the U.S. institutions appear to be granting one subset of it – Judeo-Christian traditions – increasing protection. While there may be good arguments for these kinds of jurisprudential shifts when a minority group requires protection from majoritarian tyranny, it is hard to take such arguments seriously when the Court spends page after page

---

[20] "In U.S., Decline of Christianity Continues at Rapid Pace," *Pew Research Center*, Oct. 17, 2019,
https://www.pewresearch.org/religion/2019/10/17/in-u-s-decline-of-christianity-continues-at-rapid-pace/.

[21] "Being Christian in Western Europe," *Pew Research Center*, May 29, 2018,
https://www.pewresearch.org/religion/2018/05/29/being-christian-in-western-europe/.

[22] Ross Douthat, "The Overstated Collapse of American Christianity," *The New York Times*, Oct. 29, 2019, https://www.nytimes.com/2019/10/29/opinion/american-christianity.html.

[23] Peter Beinart, "Breaking Faith," *The Atlatnic*, Apr. 2017,
https://www.theatlantic.com/magazine/archive/2017/04/breaking-faith/517785/.

recounting the prominent place of faith in American historical development; faith gets protected both because it is an unassailable tradition and because it is threatened by changes in public thought. There is no room for discussion with that sort of logic.

This book aims not to wade into the morass of First Amendment religious jurisprudence; there is no exit strategy for such discussions. Nor do I intend to argue whether the U.S. Constitution or any governing document should protect religious belief. Instead, the cases I have recounted raise important questions about public thought. And events like the Coleman murders should illustrate the urgency of such questions. How should a religious moderate or a secularist navigate public debates about religious liberty? What ethos or set of principles should guide a person, an organization, or a state through what will inevitably be a century of religious conflict? As the momentum toward secularization builds, how should a non-zealot react? If constitutional liberties and rights are protections from government interference, then the decision to enforce one set of such protections over that of others is a value judgment on the part of a society. And as these value-judgments favorable to religion proliferate, the constitution will continue to subsidize one form of behavior (religious belief) over others (personal liberties, equal access, and individual identity) during a time of religious/secular conflict.

4. Enter Apatheism

This book will offer one preliminary answer to these questions. I hope to provide a conceptual framework for those who are irreligious to think through the coming decades of change, both in terms of private commitments and public policies. In this book, I will develop a set of guiding principles under the label "apatheism," a term I will borrow, redefine, and defend. My thesis is essentially this: apatheism is a philosophical attitude, rather than a belief-system or claim to knowledge, that allows religious moderates and secularists (1) on the one hand, to feel a measure of protection for their religious beliefs (such as they are), while (2) on the other hand, to defend their view of a society that does not elevate religious liberty above that of other social goods. While some of these concepts are not new, my purpose is to bring them under one rubric for application and debate. I will first offer a sketch of what I understand apatheism to be. In the chapters to follow, I will expand the concepts and implications that I present here.

I am not the first to discuss the term apatheism. Trevor Hedberg, currently a postdoctoral scholar at Ohio State University, has perhaps the earliest and most thorough account of the practical implications of apatheism as a full-fledged philosophy. Jonathan Rauch, a senior fellow at the Brookings Institute, has noted that apatheism promises to be a helpful guiding principle in an increasingly secularized society. Moreover, there are glimmers of apatheistic beliefs in Enlightenment philosophers, such as Kant and Rousseau. So, in many ways, I am not covering wholly new ground.

At the same time, apatheism is undertheorized. No writer, to my knowledge, has yet to provide a precise definition of the philosophical position. While Hedberg has given an excellent defense of its pragmatic quality, we need a foundation from which to generate greater dialogue on what may prove to be an important subject in the coming decades. To that end, my working definition of apatheism is as follows: *Apatheism is the philosophical attitude of indifference and reciprocity, both public and private, to (1) the question of the existence of a deity, (2) the interaction of that deity with the universe, and/or (3) the value of loyalty to that deity.*

This definition is just a starting point. In order to make it clear what apatheism means, I will spend the remaining chapters breaking down each portion of this definition in the following four ways:

a) *Philosophical Attitude of Indifference*: As I discuss below, apatheism is not a claim to knowledge or belief. Rather, it is attitudinal: how does one feel about deity instead of how one thinks about deity. Apatheism treats these two sets of cognitive experiences as distinct. Moreover, as we will see, the root of apatheism is indifference. This is neither positive nor negative. Apatheism's main thrust is to meet the various questions about deity with total disinterest. At the same time, apatheism does not have to be non-confrontational or passive. One can be aggressively indifferent or argue for normative reasons behind indifference. Indeed, apatheists might have every reason to defend and advocate for their position. But when it comes to belief in deity, an apatheist shrugs.

b) *Reciprocity Public and Private*: Apatheism can have both a public and private impact in the way in which it treats others. As a political theorist, I see apatheism as both a highly individual attitude and a collective attitude of a community that essentially boils down to reciprocity. Private apatheism is the apatheism that individuals display in their personal relationships: family, friends, colleagues, and so forth. Public apatheism is the apatheism that groups and states display in their communal relationships: citizens, corporations, governments, and so forth. In every instance, apatheism does not carve out for itself special exemptions or treat itself as exceptional.

c) *The "Big Three"*: My definition includes three subjects to which apatheism can be directed: the existence of a deity, a deity's interaction with the known universe, and loyalty to deity. Not all three of these are required to "be an apatheist," and an individual apatheist might display varying degrees of indifference to all or any of the three subjects. But each of the three subjects is a matter that is ripe for an apatheistic attitude.

5. Conclusion

As I have said, this chapter is only a sketch. In later chapters, I intend to take a much deeper dive into the definition I have laid out above. I will also discuss the practical effects of apatheism, building on the work that others have already started. To reiterate, my overall goal in this project is to give an account of what I believe many individuals are feeling and are likely to feel as the topic of religious freedom continues to take up so much of our time – politically and culturally.

From Intensity to Indifference

A zealous man in religion is pre-eminently a man of one thing. It is not enough to say that he is earnest, hearty, uncompromising, thorough-going, whole-hearted, fervent in spirit. He sees one thing, he cares for one thing, he lives for one thing, he is swallowed-up in one thing – and that one thing is to please God.
– J. C. Ryle

1. In the Beginning…

I'll never forget that ride home from church services at our congregation ("ward" in Mormon-speak). The time of year is hard to pin down, but I do remember that I was 12 years old: right at that age when the small world you've lived in as a child starts to be replaced by the bigger, more complicated teen world, with the even bigger, scarier world of adulthood in the distance. I was in the backseat of my parents' car. I can't remember if my two siblings and my mother were there, but I do know that my father was driving. We had just left the parking lot of the small Mormon church house in Bern, Idaho, that my ancestors had built when they left Switzerland and Denmark in the 1860s-70s to join the Mormon movement in the American West. We were starting the short drive up the road to our home at the top of the hill. The route would take us past the homes of my paternal aunts and uncles, my cousins and second cousins and third cousins, past the first home built in Bern by my great-great grandfather where my great-grandfather, grandfather, and father had all been raised, past the tall monument outside this home that commemorated the founding of my 150-person Mormon hometown in rural Southeast Idaho.

As we left the parking lot, I was amped up about something I had been taught during one of the classes at church over the last several weeks. Church services were three hours long, and the final class was (at least for us boys) dedicated to teaching us about the "priesthood" we had been endowed with when we turned 12. Mormons believe god ("Heavenly Father") gave power to Jesus's apostles to do the work of ministering the gospel to proselytes, healing the sick, administering the sacred rites ("ordinances"), and so forth. But Mormons believe that that power was lost when the original apostles were martyred and that – despite whatever some dude in a funny hat in The Vatican might believe – it was lost for centuries due to mankind's wickedness in killing Jesus ("the Great Apostasy"). When Joseph Smith saw a vision of Heavenly Father and Jesus Christ in 1820, he was told that he would bring this power back to the world to prepare mankind for Jesus' Second Coming and final judgment. Mormons believe that Smith and his then-assistant, Oliver Cowdery, received two important visits from heavenly beings to restore this power: a visit from John the Baptist in May 1829 restoring the lesser, Aaronic priesthood and a visit at a later, unknown time by Peter, James, and John restoring the higher, Melchizedek priesthood. Since then, a line of authority had passed from Smith to his apostles to the later presidents of the Mormon church ("prophets"), regional and local leaders of the church ("stake presidents" and "bishops"), and down to every male (except Black men until a revelation in 1978) who met the necessary age and morality requirements.

At age 12, all of my peers in the ward and I had been inducted ("ordained") deacons in the Aaronic priesthood, later to be ordained teachers (age 14) and priests (age 16). At this age, our responsibilities as deacons were mostly to pass the Mormon version of the Eucharist ("the sacrament") to congregants each Sunday. But we were promised that, over time and little by little, Heavenly Father would give us greater and greater responsibilities and our priesthood power would grow. The culmination of the Aaronic priesthood preparation would be our ordination into the Melchizedek priesthood at age 18 and our selection ("calling") as a missionary for the Mormon church at age 19. Until then, the Aaronic priesthood program involved, at minimum, regular church attendance and participation in the 45-minute meetings ("quorum meetings") at the end of services. There each age group – deacon, teacher, priest – would meet with their youth ministers ("priesthood leaders") and receive standardized, Church-approved instruction that ranged from lessons about general morality to lessons about Mormon doctrine.[24]

---

[24] My understanding is that some of the organizational features I had grown up with as a Mormon priesthood holder have now changed. From what I can tell, those details are minor. For more information, see "Priesthood" in *Gospel Topics*, ChurchofJesusChrist.org,
https://www.churchofjesuschrist.org/study/manual/gospel-topics/priesthood?lang=eng.

My ride home with my family had come on the tail end of one such meeting. I can't remember every detail of the lesson during that particular deacon's quorum meeting, but I do remember what it was about and know the details from the subsequent years of having it repeated back to me. We were being taught a series of lessons on Heavenly Father's plan for saving humans from sin and bringing them back to live with and live like him ("the Plan of Salvation" or "the Plan of Happiness").

Mormons believe that all humans that have ever lived or ever will live were conceived by Heavenly Father and existed as disembodied spirits before birth ("the Preexistence"). How long we were there, how we were conceived, and why an eternal being would do this to begin with are questions that are not fully fleshed out in Mormon doctrine. What is clear is that we were given our first lessons on spirituality and gained knowledge from being in Heavenly Father's presence. Eventually god told all his children that they had progressed as far as they could and that if they wanted to be like him, they would need to follow a plan that he had prepared for them. He was perfect, immortal, and the complete fusion of a spiritual and physical body. We, at that time, were merely embryos of him, existing only in spirit form and with much less knowledge.

His plan, in a nutshell, involved our being born into mortality – literally fusing our preexistent sprits with mortal, physical bodies the mortal conception – and having our minds wiped of our premortal life ("the Veil") as we enter mortality. While behind this veil, our mortal life was intended to be a test wherein we were faced with a range of challenges from birth to death – sin, pain, pleasure, suffering, distraction, etc. We would inevitably become wicked and sinful; Heavenly Father knew that the first humans, Adam and Eve, would start a domino effect of sin. Mormonism teaches a version of original sin in that "natural man is an enemy to God, and has been from the fall of Adam, and will be, forever and ever, unless he yields to the enticings of the Holy Spirit."[25] That meant that there was no way that we could return to Heavenly Father's presence, since the minute we were born, sin would find its way into our lives. After all, *he* was perfect, sinless, and pure, and we could not exist in the same space as him if we were so sinful. Even one small imperfection would keep us out of his presence.

If the Plan had stopped there, it wouldn't be much of plan. But Heavenly Father had a solution to this problem, too. He told us that one among us would be chosen to be the vicarious sinner – the person who would take our sins from us and be punished on our behalf. This person would lead a perfect life and be completely entitled to return to Heavenly Father's presence, but he would voluntarily be punished anyway on our behalf. He, sinless and pure, would stand between us and the sword of justice. This person would also be Heavenly Father's incarnation on Earth and deliver a program ("the Gospel") whereby, if we followed his instructions, he would intercede on our behalf with Heavenly Father and demand that we be included in his heaven. In other words, by following this person and doing as he instructed, we could be included in the list of people who had their sins taken from them.

---

[25] The Book of Mormon, Mosiah 3:19.

Heavenly Father then asked all of us – all humanity – which of us would voluntarily take on this burden. Two came forward. One, Lucifer, said that he would do the task and would see to it that not a single soul would be lost. He promised that every one of Heavenly Father's children would come back home. But his condition was that *he* would be given the glory and power for doing that work, not Heavenly Father. The other, Jehovah, said he would also willingly take on this burden, but he would not constrain anyone to follow him – meaning there was the possibility that many if not all of Heavenly Father's children would not return home. Jehovah also promised to give the glory to Heavenly Father and not keep it for himself. Heavenly Father selected Jehovah, leading Lucifer to become angry and openly rebel against this plan.

Heavenly Father punished Lucifer and those of our brothers and sisters who followed him by casting them out of Heaven and sending them into the world as disembodied spirits. There they would become Satan and his demons, hellbent (literally) on thwarting the Plan. He chose Jehovah to lead Heavenly Father's children by being born into mortality through a process of spiritual conception ("overshadowing") with Heavenly Father and one of his mortal, female children. This "virgin," defined as someone who never knew a *mortal* man, would mother Jesus, who would teach the Gospel, suffer in Gethsemane for humanity's sins, die, conquer death, and return to immortality. All that humanity had to do was hear Jesus' words, believe them, do them, and all would be well – no matter how sinful they had been. And though this Gospel and the priesthood that administered it would disappear at various wicked points in human history, it would return in its fullness on the eve of Jesus' triumphant Second Coming. The founding of the Mormon church by Smith was that doctrinal return of the gospel in the Last Days ("the Restoration"). It was a risky Plan, and all of it hinged on whether Jesus really could be the Christ he was supposed to be.

As a 12-year-old young man, this felt like it was "new" to me, even if it had been repeated by whole life. Hearing it then, just as I transitioned into my teen years, was a wonderful, eye-opening lesson for a young mountain boy in a rural Western community. I'm sure that my parents and other church leaders had taught elements of this story to me before, but this was perhaps the first time that it "sunk in." But the part that stood out most to me was what came *after* – the part of the Plan that clarified mankind's final destination. Mormons believe that when we die, our spirits are once again separated from our bodies and are sent to a kind of holding place, a waiting room. There, those who had followed the Gospel in mortal life would be housed in a corner of this space called Paradise, while those who were wicked or ignorant of the Gospel would be in another corner called Prison. This space would still be tied to the Earth; Mormons believe that the spirits of the dead exist around us, separated only by our mortal, physical shells. And these spirits would still be behind the Veil and still be given a chance to accept the Gospel; the righteous in Paradise would proselyte to the ignorant in Prison. But there they would sit for centuries.

At some point in the future, when the time for Earth was up and the final days had come, Jesus would return. He would bring with him all of the dead and change both the living and returned dead into immortal beings ("the Resurrection"). All of mankind that had chosen to come to Earth – whether good or evil – would be given immortal bodies as a free gift for Jesus' conquering death in the three days that followed his crucifixion. But this free gift came with a price. Once resurrected, they would be sorted according to their commitment to the Gospel ("Judgment Day"). At that point, the Veil would be lifted, and humanity would have a full picture of themselves before and during mortality. After this judgement, all of mankind would be sent to one of four places.

- Those who refused to follow the Gospel when it was presented to them and those who lived wickedly would be sent to the lowest kingdom of salvation ("the Telestial Kingdom," a word that Smith came up with to describe it). They will have spent centuries before the Resurrection suffering Heavenly Father's wrath for failing to pass the test. But once this punishment was over and Jesus returned, this kingdom would be a beautiful resting place for them. It's unclear what this resting place would be like. Smith described it like the brightness of the stars and wonderful beyond human comprehension. What is clear is that the inhabitants would go on to be servants of Heavenly Father and of those who pass the test.
- Those who lived honorable lives and those who were blinded from the truth by erring philosophies would be sent to the middle kingdom of salvation ("the Terrestrial Kingdom"). This kingdom would be bright like the moon and even better than the Telestial Kingdom. Once again,

the only part that is clear is that the inhabitants would be servants of Heavenly Father and those who pass the test.
- Those who lived every word of the Gospel and did exactly as Jesus asked, constantly repenting of their sins, constantly checking their thoughts, words, and deeds, and, above all, *truly* loving Heavenly Father, would be sent to the highest kingdom of salvation ("the Celestial Kingdom"). This kingdom would be bright like the sun and more wonderful than the lower two. Within this kingdom, there would be three levels based on receiving ordinances in mortal life. The highest level was for those who had obtained every saving ordinance and who were married in a temple. These very special, god-like children would be given the power to "be like Heavenly Father" and live the kind of immortal life that he lives. Mormon doctrine is not totally clear on what this entails, but Smith and the Mormon prophets who came after him have generally hinted that its some form of godhood ("Exaltation"). Whether that's literal or figurative is unclear.
- For those who would have been entitled to the Celestial Kingdom but who rejected Exaltation – who openly rebelled against Jesus and Heavenly Father – would join Satan and his demons in Outer Darkness. It would be as if they never took the test in the first place. Their ultimate fate is once again unclear, but the general consensus in

Mormon doctrine is that they will eventually be destroyed, either literally or figuratively.[26]

Beyond this basic framework, Mormonism teaches that there are some important caveats to the end of humanity. First, nearly every human, no matter how evil, will be given a portion of salvation and live in some kind of "heaven" for eternity as a reward for even taking the test in the first place. Pick your favorite villain – Hitler, Dahmer, Vlad the Impaler – and they are likely headed for the Telestial Kingdom to enjoy some kind of heaven. Granted, they will suffer Heavenly Father's wrath in the spiritual holding cell after death; Prison will be an awful torture for any who are on the wrong side of the Gospel. But that punishment won't be endless. There is a kind of comfort in knowing that no matter what, post-mortality eventually won't be so bad – you may just have to spend it with a (punished) Hitler.

Second, those in the Terrestrial and Telestial Kingdoms will never again be in the presence of Heavenly Father – forever. They may enjoy his Holy Spirit (in the Telestial Kingdom) or visits from Jesus (in the Terrestrial Kingdom), and they have the distinct honor of working for Heavenly Father for eternity through a celestial chain of command. But they will never again be in Heavenly Father's presence as they were in pre-mortality. Even those in the lower levels of the Celestial Kingdom will not fully

---

[26] I believe I have presented a fair and accurate account of these Mormon doctrines as they were taught to and by me in the 30 years I was a Mormon. However, you can review these and other doctrines and draw your own conclusions. See, e.g., "Plan of Salvation," *Gospel Topics*, ChurchofJesusChrist.org, https://www.churchofjesuschrist.org/study/manual/gospel-topics/plan-of-salvation?lang=eng.

enjoy the rewards that Heavenly Father had planned for them. After all, the whole point of the Plan was to prepare mankind to be like him – anything short of that is a kind of failure. Because the Veil is gone in eternity, every human will know this– know what they were in pre-mortality, what they believed and did in mortality, and what they could have been in post-mortality. That awful knowledge will be with them forever.

These two facts imply much of the post-mortal world will be some measure of Heaven *and* some measure of Hell. Although each final destination has its positives, only those at the very top of the Celestial Kingdom will really, truly be in Heaven – Exalted and in the presence of Heavenly Father. And, Mormonism teaches, their reward is endless. Only the Exalted will be able to go on to whatever progress he has in store for them in the eons that follow. It's not clear how much of humanity will get there. After all, by some estimates, there have been 117 billion humans that have ever lived in the last 200,000 years. In Mormonism, this figure only represents that two-thirds of Heavenly Father's children that chose to follow Jehovah into mortality; another third (about 60 billion souls, by this math) are already damned for all eternity for following Lucifer. But even among that 117 billion, Mormonism generally suggests that the number of people who accept the Gospel in this life or in the Prison that follows death will probably be small. Thus, it's entirely possible that the vast majority of Heavenly Father's children will never, *ever* be allowed back in his home. Much of a Mormon's day to day life is spent doing everything possible to avoid that fate and be in the Exalted few.

Third, and perhaps most importantly, Mormonism sees itself as a *really* big deal with eternal impact. It's often difficult for Protestant Christians to really understand what is at stake for a Mormon. Mormonism is not founded in some fundamental disagreement with Catholicism. It's not a different way of assembling the pieces of a religion that reasonable minds can disagree on. Mormons don't see themselves as Lutherans or Baptists or Methodists or even Evangelical Christians do: sharing the same Christian faith with others, albeit with different emphases.

It's much, much more than that for a Mormon. If, as Mormonism teaches, the Gospel was lost from wickedness, but Heavenly Father has restored every saving truth through Smith, then Mormonism is the best news to hit humanity in 2000 years. Everything since the last apostle died in the First Century has been pointless and grasping for truth in the dark. Without that priesthood – Aaron and Melchizedek – on earth, every baptism, sacrament, rite, marriage, ceremony, etc., has zero eternal significance. It's a charade. But now that the priesthood is back – wielded by men from age 12 on up – all humans now have a chance to escape an eternity of knowing that you could have been and had more. Failure to believe Mormonism has real, vital ramifications for the destiny of one's soul after mortality – not just academic disagreement. And those ramifications are eternal.

Why, then, would someone *not* follow Mormonism? Why would someone who was born into a Mormon home in a Mormon community, with a long line of Mormon ancestors, *not* get on their knees and thank Heavenly Father ever day of their lives for this great blessing? Why would that person *not* want to go out into the world and declare bold, nobly that Mormonism is the path to salvation? And why would that person *not* use every possible means imaginable to spread this Gospel since the end result was clearly for the good of all humanity? It's a tremendous gift – a chance of a lifetime – to save yourself and everyone around you from an eternity of failure. What an honor to be counted among the elect!

It was *this* fact that hit me like a freight train that afternoon on the way home from church. I distinctly remember leaning forward and positioning myself over the middle console of the front seat of my parents' car. I vividly can see myself holding my father's old missionary copy of *A Marvelous Work and A Wonder*, a book that walks the reader in more detail through the short doctrinal lesson I've just recounted. I can hear the eagerness in my voice as I asked my dad in the driver's seat, "Did you know this?! Did you know what we believe?! We could become like a god!" For my father, it was probably just another ride home from church. This was second nature to him at this point in his life. For me, though, this has always been a pivotal moment – *the* moment when Mormonism was no longer the church I attended or the belief of my parents. It was *my belief*. It was all I needed. It was *everything*.

And I was going to do everything I could to make it my lodestar...

2. Beliefs versus Attitudes

This story is meant to highlight a distinction that I hope to make clear as part of my discussion of apatheism. This early and pivotal moment for me as a young Mormon captures two often-conflated concepts. In the previous chapter, I offered a definition of apatheism that I will discuss more fully in the next chapter. But it's at this point that one might ask what distinguishes apatheism from some of the other "-theisms" that a person might adopt? Is it just agnosticism by a different name? Some form of atheism? Is it opposition to theistic claims? The answer to these questions depends on understanding the two concepts at work in my story: belief vs. attitude.

Standard discussions of god and religious matters revolve around the degree of one's belief. "Do you believe in god?" is often seen as the fundamental question in any would-be discussion of religion in private and public life. It does not require elaboration to point out that there are varying degrees of affirmative or negative responses to this question. Ask yourself that question right now: Do you believe in god. Your answer will range along a spectrum – an X-axis for the more math-oriented among us. On the right side of that spectrum, the positive side, are affirmative answers; individual beliefs that in some way declare, "Yes, there is a god" can be plotted on the right side. On the left side of that spectrum, the negative side, are denials of that question; beliefs that declare, "No, there is no god" can plotted on the left.

Yes or no answers to that question are valid and often a simple way to begin a theological discussion. But few of us have beliefs that function like an on and off switch, and religious beliefs are great examples of this fact. The "Yes" answers can display degrees of belief. For example, the most positive claims about god fall under the heading *theism*, which holds that not only is there a god, but that god is personal, involved in humanity, and can intervene in our affairs (through prayer, for example). Such beliefs are strong affirmations. But not every believer has such strong commitments. Some, for example, may believe that there is a god but that this god is something like a force or amorphous entity. The entity may have started the universe and walked away from it. Or that entity is on a different plane of existence and therefore unreachable. Or that entity might care loosely for us when it comes to our soul, but it doesn't concern itself with our day-to-day behavior. These softer statements of affirmation fall under the heading *deism*.

You are probably starting to get the picture of how I am conceptualizing beliefs. If the left side of the spectrum is some form of negative responses to the belief question, then you can imagine that these also come by degrees. Total denials of the existence of a god or any god or denials of even wanting to have such a being exist are a form of *global atheism*: no matter the religion, no god exists. A softer version of atheism, though, holds that a particular god or particular articulations of god do not exist. The person who espouses such beliefs might be open at some point to evidence that a god exists, but, so far as the person's experience and knowledge go, the god or gods of certain religions don't exist. We can call this *local atheism*. And, since these beliefs are a spectrum, an answer to the belief question might simply be, "I don't know" or "I could be persuaded either way." This middle position of openness to evidence we can call *agnosticism*. See Figure 1 for a visual representation of these concepts.

Non Belief — Global Atheism — Local Atheism — Agnosticism — Deism — Theism — Belief

KNOWLEDGE

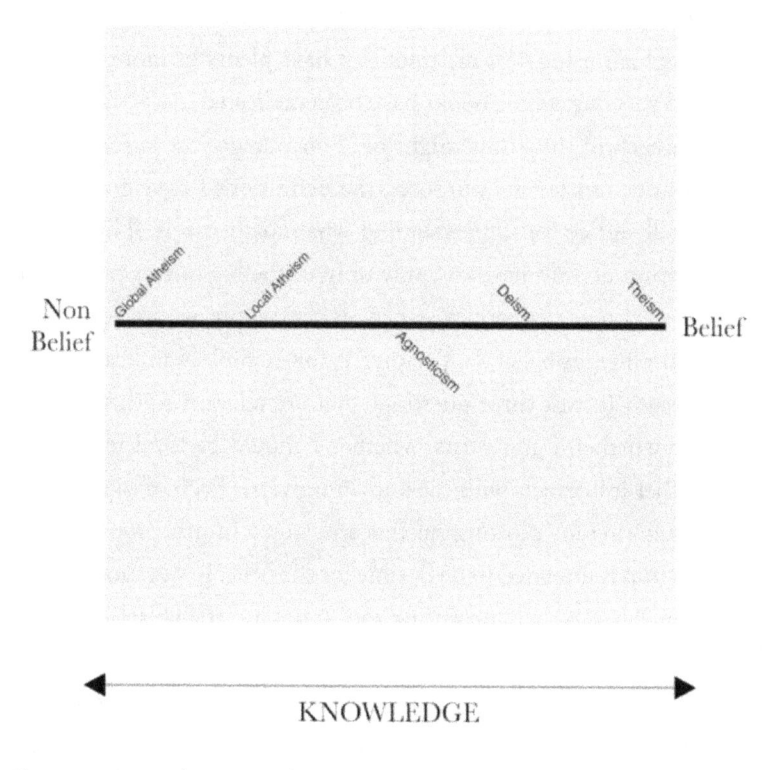

Figure 1: A one-dimensional spectrum of knowledge claims about deity

As you plot yourself on this spectrum, it's important to have in mind a few caveats. First, this spectrum is not a hierarchy. A person does not have to proceed from one point to the other as part of some faith transition. It's totally plausible, for instance, that a person could have a strong commitment to global atheism, have a spiritual awakening, and become a theist without ever transitioning through the intervening -isms. The reverse can be true as well. This spectrum is merely a helpful way to categorize beliefs, not a description of how people adjust their beliefs. Second, the terms I am using here are ones that have plenty of more complicated versions; whole books have been dedicated to discussions of what each of this -isms might be. I encourage you to read those accounts, but for my purposes, the definitions I have given thus far will suffice for understanding what apatheism is. Third, this spectrum doesn't have to apply only to the big question about a god's existence or nonexistence. It can apply to any question about religious belief. In Chapter 1, for example, I indicated that there are at least three questions that are relevant to this discussion: whether a god exists, whether I should be loyal to it, and whether it interacts with the known universe. Each of these questions is ripe for plotting on this spectrum. In other words, this spectrum is intended to be flexible for the belief in question. Once again: this is only a measuring tool – not a stone-chiseled law of nature.

Thus far, none of this is probably very new to you. If you have picked up this book, you have probably thought through this "degrees of belief" phenomenon at some point, even if you did not articulate it in the same way I have. While categorizing beliefs is definitely helpful, we are not solely a product of our beliefs. You and I may believe lots of things. We have political beliefs, economic beliefs, scientific beliefs, and so forth. But even if you and I share the same belief, we both might approach it with different degrees of interest. You can imagine, for instance, someone who shares your political beliefs but who doesn't care as much as you do about those beliefs. You might be the type who canvasses for a party, volunteers at polling locations, votes in every election, or runs for office. Your friend at work might share your same views about politics, but they may not care too much about being involved to the point that they are particularly politically active. When judged *only* from the perspective of belief, the two of you look to be identical. And yet, in practice, you are very different in how you display your beliefs.

This difference in practice can be called your attitude rather than your belief.[27] With beliefs, we ask about what a person knows or thinks they know. With attitudes, we ask about what a person feels toward those beliefs. To use an analogy, beliefs are like a car: constructed a certain way, designed to perform certain functions, and full of possibilities. But beliefs on their own are inert. Attitudes are like the fuel, the driver, the electricity that propel the car. The kind and degrees of attitudes we put in will change how that car behaves, even if the car is identical to another.

Thus, in our context, we can ask the knowledge question, "Do you believe in god?" but we might pair it with, "And how do you feel about it?" or "How much energy do you dedicate to this belief?" For us, this is an attitudinal question that tests whether or not a person cares about religious matters at all. Once again, we

---

[27] Whether this bears out in the psychological or sociological literature is a question for someone else who is better versed in those subjects than I am. As a political philosopher by day, the most I can offer is that this *seems* to be how we behave or that we *logically* behave this way. It does not really matter to my discussion whether a psychologist would see beliefs and attitudes as different concepts; in this discussion, I am making the affirmative claim from a theoretical perspective that this is how we behave and leave it to the social scientists to describe whether this theory is true.

can imagine positive and negative responses to this question and plot them on a new spectrum (a Y-axis).

On the positive side, are answers that take some form of "I care a great deal about these beliefs" or "I spend a lot of my day-to-day life motivated by these beliefs." Like the political activists, the believer here might be very active in their beliefs. We can call this type of answer *zeal* and the person who holds it a *zealot*. Zealotry likely needs no explanation; you need only read the latest news story about sectarian conflict somewhere in the world to get a sense of what zealotry is. You can easily imagine, then, someone who has a belief about god *and* who makes that fact a central part of their life. Maybe, at the furthest extreme, they are willing to die or kill for their beliefs. Or maybe they are slightly motivated to act on their beliefs: they discuss it occasionally, participate in communities of similar believers, or read literature about those beliefs.

But just like belief questions, these attitudinal questions have a negative answer as well: "I don't care much about this belief" or "It doesn't take up much of my daily life." Again, like the political person who does not actively participate in politics, the believer in this context might not stress too much about their belief or non-belief in a god, their loyalty to it, or that god's interaction with the universe. This is what I am calling *apatheism*. Just as atheism and theism arrive at opposite conclusions concerning knowledge of deity, apatheism and zeal arrive at opposite conclusions about attitude. Apatheism is equally forceful as zeal in its indifference to matters of deity. Thus, while a zealot might take the positive position that "I care a great deal about matters of god," you can imagine a hard apatheist might take the furthest negative position that "I do not care at all about matters of god."

It is crucial for the discussion that follows in subsequent chapters that you understand this distinction between belief and attitude and not let these concepts collapse together. An atheist is not automatically an apatheist – those are different terms describing different concepts in the same way that the word "red" is different from "cold." Nor are theists always zealots. Remember that these are operating on two different dimensions like an X- and Y-axis. Because attitude it is second-dimensional, apatheism (and its opposite, zeal) is consistent with the first-dimensional beliefs. So, for example, one *could* be an apatheistic atheist ("I know there isn't a god, but I don't care a great deal about such matters") or an apatheistic theist ("I know there is a god, but I don't care a great deal about such matters"). The reverse could also be true. One could be a zealot atheist ("I know there isn't a god, and I care a great deal about such matters.") or a zealot theist ("I know there is a god, and I care a great deal about such matters."). These two dimensions, when treated separately, offer a very helpful rubric for understanding how beliefs and attitudes interact with one another when a person religious claims.

To further drive home the need to treat these separately, Figure 2 gives a visual representation of what I mean. Visualizing both dimensions at once, we can begin to see how some groups might be categorized epistemically and attitudinally.

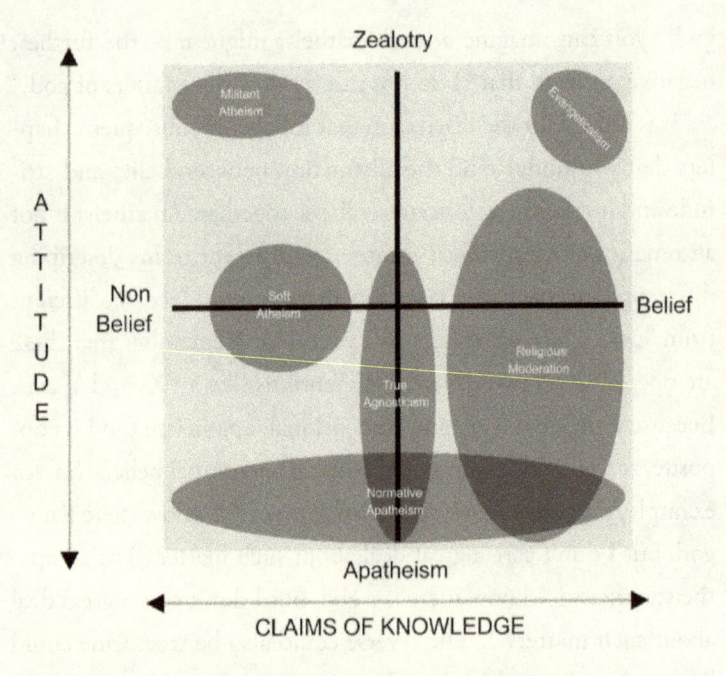

Figure 2: A two-dimensional spectrum of knowledge claims about and attitudes toward deity.

So, we might imagine a group of moderate Christians in some community in the United States. All of them share the same theistic beliefs; to them, god does exist, and he happens to be the Christian version of god. But some of these parishioners might attend church regularly each Sunday, while their fellow believers might prioritize something else, like having a restful Sunday morning or putting in overtime at work. Similarly, we might place some of the New Atheists (though, maybe not all of them) near the top left quadrant: people who are deeply convinced that there is no god of any sort in the universe and who are actively trying to convince others of this fact.

3. What Apatheism Isn't

I want to pause here to work through apatheism at this higher level before we plunge into the details in the next chapters. The categories I have made above are not hard and fast categorizations. You could probably quibble with how I have placed people on the graph in Figure 2, and to be honest, I would be open to having that discussion. But I want to stress that this is merely hypothesis, a framework to have the conversation. As I emphasized in the Preface, my goal here is not to convince you that people are one way or the other, or that apatheism is better than zealotry, or that atheism is worse than theism. Rather, the discussion above is my effort to signal how these concepts relate to one another, with the idea that we will have more precision as we work through the definition sketched out. My primary goal is to help give voice to attitudes that often disappear in our discussion of religion.

We are so fixated on the beliefs of a person that we rarely ask how committed they are to those beliefs. Or we assume that if someone is a religious person, they must automatically be a zealot. But throughout the United States and most Western countries, there is a growing body of people who are Religious Nones: people who don't identify with any religion. If we only looked at their beliefs, we would likely find a range of beliefs going from atheism to theism that would make us scratch our heads and wonder, "Well, what are these people?" I am firmly in that camp and have been confused for many years about what I am. But when we introduce attitude into the conversation it's not too hard to see what these Religious Nones are: they're apatheists, even if they might be atheists or theists or something in between. Likewise, we can survey the US population and find a sizable group of people who are very wound up about religion: Evangelical Christians, rabid secularists, Muslim extremists, Orthodox Jews, etc. These groups could not be more different in how they answer the belief questions. And yet, they all share something attitudinally. All of them display some degree of zealotry in their beliefs. And they are often much louder, and therefore get more attention, than the Religious Nones.

If the foregoing conversation is a bit too abstract and conceptual for you, then let me return to my own experience that I described earlier. Throughout this book, I will draw from my own experience to show how zealotry and apatheism relate to one another, but this first story gives a good case study in what I mean by zealotry.

When we hear the word zealotry in colloquial conversations, we probably have in mind one of the following: a passionate Evangelical Christian who pickets abortion clinics or the funerals of gay veterans, a Muslim who attacks an author for writing an article critical of Islam or an artist for drawing a picture of Muhammed, an Amish elder who threatens dissenters with exile and ostracization. The events of 9/11 are still in recent enough memory that the word zealot probably conjures up images of burning skyscrapers, exploding planes, and people throwing themselves out of windows hundreds of feet in the air. Our colloquial definition of a zealot, then, is probably some form of "a religious extremist who commits controversial if not violent acts." This colloquial definition is helpful, as it paints a vivid picture of what zealotry is. It's a good "gut check" on our intuitions.

On its own, there's nothing particularly wrong with that definition. I certainly mean *at least* that by zealotry; my definition captures the jihadist or the murderous Christian. But my definition is more expansive than just that. Take my own story. As a 12-year-old boy, my beliefs had been my beliefs for most of my childhood. I believed in the Mormon version of god. I attended church regularly. I read Mormon scriptures. I was baptized and confirmed as a Mormon when I was 8, two of the saving ordinances that the Mormon church's priesthood performs as part of the Gospel. If you had asked 8-year-old me if I believed in Mormonism, I could genuinely answer in the affirmative. I was not a unique child, either; many young Mormon boys and girls will happily declare their beliefs if you ask them. Granted, you could make a valid argument that much of this is probably reflexive training and cultural grooming, but I did not and still do not believe that totally captures my experience or that of my Mormon peers. Children, for all the development they have yet to experience, are not stupid; as a parent of a young child, I will adamantly deny that my son believes everything I tell him. For the sake of argument, take me and the other Mormon kids at our word when we say that as 8-year-olds we believed it.

But my own experience shows how incomplete that narrative is. Believing alone is only half the story. Throughout my life I encountered (and still know) hundreds if not thousands of individuals who believe in Mormonism. It's part of their identity, their culture, their community. Some of them will volunteer their beliefs to you, even when you wish they wouldn't. Others are more hidden, more introverted about their beliefs. Get them around a campfire late at night and start waxing metaphysical, and you'll start hearing them articulate their beliefs. But day to day? Probably not. Yet are they attending weekly church services, volunteering their time for the Mormon church, paying tithing, following the Gospel, etc. ("active Mormons," in Mormon-speak)? The answer is almost certainly yes. And there are still other Mormons who believe in Mormonism, who have a general commitment to it as a philosophy, and who share the same ideas as the more active Mormons. But they are not attending church or following the Gospel to the letter or talking about it to neighbors or spending every waking moment measuring themselves against the Mormon standard ("inactive Mormons").

The colloquial definition of zeal would only capture the most active Mormon and would offer nothing for us in understanding the other degrees to which one could be committed to Mormonism. Instead, a better definition of zeal would be *an attitude of exclusionary intensity with regard to religious beliefs*. Under this definition, a zealot can be a cult leader or suicide bomber, since they display an attitude of exclusion towards others and their beliefs, while still sharing a pew with someone who is less intense in their attitudes. In the context of my own prior faith, it's easier to see how groups of Mormons differ along attitudinal lines while still sharing the same beliefs. The most active, committed Mormons would be the most zealous, the least active more apatheistic, and the middle group oscillating between the two along the attitudinal Y-axis. And yet, their X-axis values might be virtually identical.

In my own case, the story I related driving home from church with my father was my moment of zealotry. Looking back, I cannot call it anything else. In the following chapters, I will add more to this story and, as you will come to see, my journey to zealot started from this crucial turning point. Up to that point, even as a child, I had believed. I would likely have continued to believe in that same way throughout my life. I have people in my life – my wife, my sister, and a few close friends – who followed that trajectory and spent most of their teenage years and early adulthood believing in a vanilla sort of way. Looking at our shared beliefs, one would think we were all in the same bucket.

But for me, this moment was a shift in attitude away from that middling energy that other Mormons in my life might have had. As I indicated above, Mormon doctrine hit me square in the face. It energized me. Mormonism gave life to *everything* I did. During my teenage years, I put off dating, attended church and Mormon seminary during high school, actively participated in priesthood activities, avoided any outward displays of immorality, and so forth. Inwardly, I was a raging ball of desire for being accepted by Heavenly Father. I wanted *desperately* to be one of his elect. I prayed daily, at times hourly. I read the Book of Mormon and other Mormon scriptures with intensity. I begged Heavenly Father to give me visions, to strengthen my priesthood power, to let me in to what I believed was an inner circle of people who Heavenly Father would make his foot soldiers in the war against Satan. Everything I did aimed toward one day being a missionary for my church. I was eager to leave home at 19, to cut myself off from my family,[28] to spend $10,000 of my parents' money, and to give two years of unpaid labor to the Mormon church's proselytizing effort. I wanted to be the best missionary that I could possibly be. And I believed that if I did that, Heavenly Father would reward me with a good life, a beautiful wife, and a big family of kids, so that I could be the steward of my ancestors' sacrifice in joining the Mormon movement.

In the two years leading up to the mission, I doubled down on my preparation. I started the first year of college at Brigham Young University-Idaho, and I ensconced myself in missionary preparation. I stopped having anything to do with girls (not that they were beating down my door anyway) to avoid any sexual sins or activity that would even get me close to those sins, like kissing or holding hands. I worked constantly to keep my thoughts clean of any impurity, to shove down the raging hormones of my adolescence. I woke up every morning at 6:00 am, read my scriptures, prayed, and headed out the door for a 7:00 am class about the Book of Mormon for preparing missionaries. I had paid 10% of my meager income to the Mormon church since I was a kid doing odd jobs and then as a teenager doing after-school jobs. But in this year, I paid more through charitable contributions. I fasted each month. I taught and served in my student ward. I met with

---

[28] At that time, missionaries were not allowed to call home except twice a year: on Christmas and Mother's Day. We were allowed to write home and could email once a week when we had a day of cleaning, laundry, and selfcare ("Preparation Day"). I believe the Mormon church has changed this practice in the age of Zoom and social media. At the same time, I believe it has lowered the age to 18 when young men are expected to serve a mission.

my ward's bishop, a former mission president, as often as I could to confess my sins and to ask for his help in making me the model missionary. I've since learned, in the various communities I've lived in throughout the United States and as a university professor, that this was not at all the typical first-year college experience. Even if I recognized that at the time, every time I stumbled upon a scripture that spoke to me or heard a talk that even vaguely touched on my experience, I took it as a sign from Heavenly Father that I was on the right path. As psychologically stressful as that year was, those little moments of affirmation were all I needed to keep going. It was the time in my life that my beliefs were fully fused with my attitude.

The pinnacle of this preparation came in May 2003 when I applied to be a missionary. I wanted to time it so that I could be as close to minimum age of 19 as I could. When I got my call to serve in Houston, Texas, I looked passed the fact that my peers were going to more far-off places like Kenya or Ukraine or Japan. To a boy from rural Idaho who had never once set foot out of the Western United States, Houston was good enough. I knew Heavenly Father was sending me to the people and place that would be prepared for me. I was honored to go preach to the confused Southern Baptists, Nondenominationals, and Evangelicals.

Once my call was in, I was entitled to take the next saving ordinances: the rituals in the Mormon temple.[29] I will never forget

---

[29] Mormons are under an oath not to disclose what happens in these rituals, as they believe they are too sacred to share. Since leaving the Mormon church, I do not hold myself to that oath any more, but I do not have the space nor interest in describing those rituals. I will only say that they are not

that day. The temple had been a distant, far-off moment as a child, but I had been taught from an early age to prepare for the temple. Eventually, I would return to the temple for the final saving ordinance – marriage. And, though I didn't foresee it at the time, by the time I was a lawyer in Washington, DC, in 2012-2015, I would be a temple worker, performing these rituals for others. But for now, like every would-be missionary, I was given the Initiatory and the Endowment to prepare me to be a "king and priest" in Heavenly Father's kingdom. Sitting next to my father and grandfather in the temple, seeing my mother across the room, and feeling the weight of the moment was my most powerful experience to that point in my life. I felt strongly that everything I had done, everything I had given up, was a small sacrifice for being here in this moment. Maybe other Mormon boys my age had taken it all in stride as just another thing Mormons do. But for me, this moment in the temple was everything. For the next several weeks, before I left for my mission the day after my 19th birthday, I returned to the temple as often as I could to meditate and prepare myself for my mission.

If you had asked me in August 2003 if I was a Mormon, you would have been hit with a passionate sermon on Mormon doctrine. I would have shed tears and told you that every part of my essence confirmed that Mormonism was the *only* path back to

---

nearly as mysterious as non-Mormons assume. Looked at from an outside perspective without the scaffolding of growing up in the Mormon church, these rituals are actually very boring, vague on the details, and, at times, a little silly. If you are interested in them, I encourage you to do your own research about them. The Internet has many resources if you are curious about the Mormon temple. I encourage you to read and view both Mormon and non-Mormon sources on this topic to get a full picture.

Heaven. Joseph Smith, as quoted by another prophet of the Mormon church, John Taylor, said something that was my primary motivation at that time:

> *You will have all kinds of trials to pass through. And it is quite as necessary for you to be tried as it was for Abraham and other men of God, and...God will feel after you, and He will take hold of you and wrench your very heart strings, and if you cannot stand it, you will not be fit for an inheritance in the Celestial Kingdom of God.*

In the quiet moments of the night before and during my mission, I would ask myself, "Would I die for this faith like the martyrs and pioneers who had come before me? Could I do what Abraham did, and offer up my only son to be sacrificed on Heavenly Father's altar?" I searched my heart to see what I was committed to. If you had asked me those questions, I would have looked you square in the eye and unblinkingly said, "Yes. Without deviation." It was against that backdrop that I left home and became a missionary.

My point in sharing this part of my life is that there is no question I was a Mormon zealot in my late-teens and early-20s. But that didn't happen overnight. My march toward the pinnacle of zealotry started right there, in the backseat of my parents' car on the way home from church. From that moment, my attitude shifted up the Y-axis, as it were. At any point from age 12 on up, you could have found evidence of zeal in my life: the tithe paying, the dietary restrictions, the increasing church attendance, etc. My beliefs alone did not do this; they started the ball rolling, but it was my attitude that changed on that ride home. If the Gospel was true with such eternal consequences, why *wouldn't* I give everything to it? *That* intensity that slowly ratcheted up is what I mean by zealotry.

4. A Zealous Apatheist?

In the next chapters, I will discuss the public and private aspects of apatheism and what I am calling the "Big Three" attitudes to which apatheism could be directed. But before turning to those discussions, I want to resolve a theoretical question that you might be asking, namely, "Can a person be a dedicated apatheist? Or does apatheism mean total apathy?" After all, if apatheism is an attitude of indifference, then wouldn't an apatheist not really care about apatheism? If someone is a zealous apatheist isn't that a contradiction of terms, like a snake eating its own tail?

These questions display a fundamental confusion about what apatheism and zealotry mean under my framework. Apatheism, like the zealotry I've described above, is *only* directed to how beliefs, or knowledge claims about god, impact a person's life. A true apatheist is only apathetic about *religious claims of knowledge*. Such a person, when asked about their beliefs, would shrug, and say that those beliefs don't hold much motivation in their lives. But the key is that it's the *beliefs* themselves that are the subject of indifference – not other questions like the purpose of life, morality, humanity's destiny, etc. As my discussion above suggests, a person might have religious beliefs that touch on all those subjects. But those religious beliefs are not necessarily definitive answers to an apatheist in the same way they are to a zealot. A zealot doesn't need any other information besides their religious beliefs to address those questions. An apatheist puts religious or non-religious beliefs in the same bucket as other sources of knowledge. Once again, religion is not given special priority to an apatheist.

This also means that apatheism cannot be apathetic toward itself either. Apatheism is not the same as apathy, and zealotry is not the same as zeal. These terms have specific meanings within my framework, which is why it is even more important to keep the colloquial definition of zeal out of this conversation. Apatheism says, "I believe/don't believe, but I'm not too worried about it" in answer to the question, "How do you feel toward god?" That is a discrete question. A totally different, normative question could then be raised, "And based on that attitude, do you think others *should* be apatheists? Is apatheism the *best* way to live?" To that question, an apatheist could emphatically say, "Yes," and still be an apatheist. Such an apatheist might be deeply committed to their apathy toward their beliefs – zealous if you need that word – but not about the beliefs *themselves*. To use our graph schematic, such questions would introduce a whole new variable: a Z-axis or third dimension. One could ask a battery of questions that would plot people on all three dimensions: belief, attitude, and normative claims. These three dimensions are as different as, say, width, height, and depth in measuring a piece of wood. Saying that depth and width are the same is to make measurement impossible and to introduce nonsense.

Granted, those additional normative questions are interesting, but they are beyond the scope of this book. As I said in the Preface, my goal here is not to persuade you to be an apatheist or to defend apatheism as the best way to live. I'm going to avoid, as often as I can, that sort of editorializing. Rather, my goal is to explain what an apatheist is and to provide an apatheist with a helpful framework for articulating their beliefs and attitudes. Cards on the table, I *do* believe that apatheism, of some sort, is preferential to, say, zealotry, and I *do* think the world would be better off (or, at least, that US politics would be better off) if more people were vocal apatheists. I hint at that toward the end of this book. I also strongly believe that this is the direction that Western society has been going for some time, and I will gladly sit around any table (preferably with a bottle of wine and a good meal) to discuss those views. In that sense, I answer in the affirmative on normative questions.

But my immediate point with this discussion is to head off any criticism that apatheism is self-defeating or paradoxical. I often hear such criticisms among students and scholars in political theory ("Isn't liberty as a principle of politics self-defeating and paradoxical? Isn't that why the Weimar Republic produced Nazis?"). I find that these sorts of critiques are usually very confused about basic definitions and are often constructed around straw man versions of the ideas they are critiquing ("Liberty means absolute freedom, so how come the state can use force to protect liberty?"). They are the sort of arguments you have to address in the first week of a semester because someone in the back of the room thinks they are cleverer than everyone else. Such arguments are already destined to fail since the speaker is using two different definitions for the same concept and trying to act like they aren't doing so. In our present context, do not fall into the semantic trap that an apatheist is never, ever zealous in their life or that zealots are never ever apathetic about the zealotry of others. The burden of proof is on a critic to show me why someone cannot, rationally, be a vocal apatheist or to show why apatheism towards beliefs leads to apathy towards attitudes. Until one can make that case using the terms as I've defined them and play on my ballfield, I don't see how such claims are anything but deeply confused and not worthy of my or your time.

Reciprocity: Private and Public

The Lord told me it's flat none of your business.
– Jimmy Swaggart, to his congregation, after being
found with a prostitute

1. We'll Sing and We'll Shout with the Armies of Heaven

It was a warm, late-winter day in 2005 in Beaumont, Texas, and I can definitively say that I had snapped. I was a little over six months away from being done with my mission. In August, I would be released, having "served honorably," and I was looking forward to my return home, to continue school at BYU-Idaho, and to – above all – find someone to marry in the temple. To this point, I had been as successful a missionary as I believed I possibly could have been, while at the same time feeling that there was so much more I had not done. And, finally, my pressure valve had popped.

Up to that point, my experience had been typical of other missionaries. After leaving the Missionary Training Center ("MTC") in Provo, Utah, in August 2003 and arriving in Houston that September, I had "hit the ground running." I had spent years preparing for this experience, and I was not going to mess it up. When I was handed my copy of the Missionary Handbook – a small, white, pocket-sized book that contained the rules of missionary service – I had taken it as my personal commandment from Heavenly Father. This was my law, my constitution.

Before serving and while in the MTC, I routinely met with the bishop of my ward for worthiness interviews. The questions were often probing of my beliefs, my commitment to the Mormon church, and my morality. Did I believe that Joseph Smith was a prophet? Did I believe President So-And-So was the current prophet? Did I believe the Book of Mormon was a true book of scripture? Had I had sex with anyone, looked at pornography, masturbated, or engaged in any "heavy petting" with another person? Did I pay my tithing and restrict my diet to approved foods and drinks? From age 12 all the way up to the moment I left the MTC for Houston, I answered these and other questions multiple times a year – in the MTC, weekly. And I was proud to look my bishop in the eye and satisfactorily answer each question.

While in the mission, our leadership hierarchy ensured that the Missionary Handbook and moral principles were followed to the letter. We lived with at least one fellow missionary ("our companion") and were never to be alone without them. Your companion was selected by the mission president – a person chosen directly by the leadership in Salt Lake City and the primary authority in a mission. The mission president, through prayerful consideration and revelation, would pair you with the person who (we were told) was best for you at that time, the person with whom the Lord wanted you to be. About every three months or so, we could expect a new companionship, and every six months or so, we could expect a transfer to a new geographic area somewhere within our mission. Individual companionships were responsible for a small area, two or three areas made a district, two or three districts made a zone, and about ten areas made a mission. Some missionaries were chosen ("called") to serve as leaders of districts and zones, while within individual companionships one missionary was given some authority over the other (the "senior companion"). This line of authority from companion to district leader to zone leader to the mission president ensured that each companionship had multiple leaders to report to and that reports would be properly made from the bottom to the top of the mission. In short, it was impossible to violate a rule without at least one other person knowing about it.

My own mission president – a former Marine and corporate executive and the highest authority in my mission of about 300 missionaries – had added to these standard rules in a variety of ways. There were language constraints, like not calling new missionaries "greenies" and only referring to one another by our titles ("Elder Kunz," not "Adam" or just "Kunz"). There were media constraints, like a ban on listening to any music that wasn't an officially produced song by the Mormon church or reading any literature that was not an official Church publication – even if it was written by a Mormon author. There were severe rules about being near or talking to the opposite sex. And there were mandatory benchmarks we were required to report for the work we had done in a week: a certain number of hours we spent knocking on doors ("tracting"), visiting with Mormons about proselytizing their non-Mormon friends ("referrals"), and pairing with local priesthood leaders ("exchanges") to visit inactive Mormons (the approved term was "less actives") and prospective converts.

There were also rules about our daily schedule, some of which missionaries throughout the world followed and some of which were idiosyncratic for my particular mission. Our days started at 6:30 am, with time for breakfast, individual scripture study, scripture study with our companion, and morning planning and prayer. We were to be out of our apartment no later than 9:30 am and, other than a short lunch around noon, we were expected to be working full-time until 9:30 pm. Even dinners at 6:00 pm were intended to be time spent eating with Mormons in our area who could give us referrals to their non-Mormon or less active friends. When the day was done, we were expected to plan for the next day, end our activities with personal and companionship prayer, and be in bed no later than 10:30 pm. This was the schedule seven days a week, with one day (Wednesday) abbreviated by a few hours to give us time for laundry, emailing family, and running errands.

Our lives were austere. Although my parents had paid $10,000 to the Mormon church for my privilege to serve a mission (funds that were intended to cover the cost of housing), my monthly living allowance was less than $150. Whatever needs I had that weren't covered by this allowance were supposed to be donated by local Mormons. My mission president expected us to be in full suit and tie at all times, though we were allowed to remove our suit jacket while outdoors during the brutally hot and humid Houston summers. In my first area, our sole means of transportation was bikes, while in large areas I would serve in later, my companion and I shared a vehicle. It was a requirement to report to the mission office each month the number of miles we had used with odometer readings; if we went beyond that monthly mileage allotment, we could have the vehicle taken away.

I have had people unfamiliar with Mormonism ask how it is possible that teenage boys would ever agree to spend two years living this lifestyle; why would anyone want to do so? And what's to stop any of them from violating any of the hundreds of rules? I often respond that the experience is as close to military as one can get without actually being a soldier. The reality is that for me and many of my peers this two years of service was an honor. After all, Mormonism was the *only* true religion in the world, and, as I have already demonstrated in the previous chapter, the eternal stakes for people were enormously high. After my religious awakening at age 12, I was told over and over by every Mormon adult that there is no greater honor than serving as a missionary – that no time in my life will compare to the rich, spiritual experience of sacrificing everything for Heavenly Father. Moreover, it was a commandment! The prophets before I was born and every prophet during my life had said that *every* worthy and able young man should serve a mission (young women were not expected to do so, as motherhood was primarily their mission, though they were nevertheless encouraged). If I hadn't served a mission, I would be defying Heavenly Father and risk jeopardizing my exaltation. I would bring shame to all the people who had come before me, who had sacrificed all they had to rear me in the Mormon church. The handful of young men I knew who didn't serve a mission, either voluntarily or because they were not worthy to do so, were often looked down on or shunned by the community. Young women were often encouraged not to date or marry a young man who hadn't served a mission. Leadership and activity in the Mormon church was often tied to whether a person had served a mission. While there is no official policy in the Mormon church to treat non-missionaries in this way, the cultural mentality of Idaho and Utah makes it the norm. In short, not only was it an honor to be a missionary, but it was also a default expectation in my society.

But as prepared and committed as I was, leaving Idaho and coming to Houston was the most eye-opening experience in Mormonism that I had to that date for at least two reasons. First, I had expected that every young man had prepared the same way I had; I soon found out that they had not. There were missionaries who didn't keep to the daily schedule, those that contacted home when they weren't allowed, those that left their areas to go to theme parks or shopping malls. There were missionaries who had relationships with local young women. Within the first week of my mission, I was shocked to find that even my first companion (my "trainer") wouldn't follow the most basic of rules. I'd later see this sort of laxness even among some mission leaders – young men I looked up to – who had slacked off with their daily schedule or with the media they were consuming. It wasn't so much that I thought these individuals were sinners, as it was that I couldn't understand why they would want to do anything else but follow the rules. What a waste of time to be a missionary and do it poorly!

Second, I was not at all prepared for the fact that the people of southeast Texas were not eager to hear from Mormons. I knew enough of the South, the "Bible Belt," and born-again

Christianity to not be deluded; I didn't expect converting anyone would be easy. But I was not prepared for the overt hostility. There were moments of aggression: being angrily yelled at while on someone's front porch, being mocked while walking or biking through the streets, or being told regularly that we were devil worshipers. There were more violent moments, too. I was shot at once by a paint ball gun (a hit), once by a potato launcher (a miss), and once by a wrist rocket sling shot (a hit). Another time, I was hit by a glass beer bottle that was thrown out the window of a passing car, which didn't result in much more than some bruises. Yet another time, my companion and I couldn't get into our apartment and, when I attempted to open a window by our porch, the glass shattered, slicing up each of the fingers in my right hand. When we tried to get help from our downstairs neighbor, he told me to "go bleed to death for all I care." But the aggression and violence were the exception, not the norm. Instead, the daily experience was one of silent ridicule and dislike, peppered occasionally by a kind person who would offer a meal, a glass of water, and a few minutes in an air-conditioned living room.

Oddly, none of this diminished my commitment to missionary service. As the weeks turned to months, my initial shock turned to greater resolve. When I found examples of "lukewarm" missionaries, I told myself that it as a moral lesson: I wasn't going to be like "those missionaries." The Lord had promised me, and my mission president confirmed it, that if I would follow the simple rules, I would be entitled to greater blessings and greater rewards, so that when the big rules came, I would be prepared. How could Heavenly Father trust me with his priesthood power and, someday, the power of godhood, if I couldn't even follow a dress code or daily schedule as a missionary? The rules made sense to me on a cosmic level, and I assure you – having known some highly committed missionaries – that I was not alone in that thinking.

Moreover, the local hostility only confirmed what I already knew in my heart: that I was on the Lord's errand. Missionaries often sang Mormon hymns about missionary service, with names like "Called to Serve" and "Ye Elders of Israel," rousing songs that lifted the spirit. My own go-to hymn was "The Spirit of God," with its Mormon eschatology and promise of building "Zion":

> *We'll call in our solemn assemblies in spirit,*
> *To spread forth the kingdom of heaven abroad,*
> *That we through our faith may begin to inherit*
> *The visions and blessings and glories of God.*
> *We'll sing and we'll shout with the armies of heaven,*
> *Hosanna, hosanna to God and the Lamb!*
> *Let glory to them in the highest be given,*
> *Henceforth and forever, Amen and amen!*[30]

The fact that people opposed my beliefs so vehemently was proof that I was right. They had persecuted prophets and saints in every era of human interaction with god. My Savior had endured the most awful abuses in the name of Heavenly Father. My

---

[30] "The Spirit of God," *Hymns of The Church of Jesus Christ of Latter-day Saints* (Salt Lake City, UT: Intellectual Reserve, Inc., 1985), Hymn No. 2.

prophet, Joseph Smith, had been butchered in a jail in Missouri. My ancestors had sold their possessions in Europe, moved to the American West, and struggled for a foothold in a mountain desert, all for god. Was I greater than any of them? No. I would knock on every door, I would speak to every person, and I would try to convert every soul I could find to Mormonism – because I was a representative of Heavenly Father and his message mattered.

Believe me when I say that every event that happened to me during those first 18 months was a sign to me that I was either on the right path or straying from it. On the one hand, I had some early, quasi-successes: befriending a man married to a Mormon woman, who just needed a surrogate son to feel whole, teaching scripture study to local Mormons preparing for missions, and giving my time for community service. I had also served in leadership positions: a trainer for a new missionary in my first transfer, a district leader, a zone leader, and, in July 2004, as one of two assistants to our mission president. Granted, the bulk of my service was ostensibly still missionary work, but as time had gone on, I found myself in more administrative roles, separated from the average convert. When I was called to serve as an assistant, my role shifted to helping the mission president manage a 300-person mission. My companion and I were charged with training other missionaries, overseeing zones within the mission, and serving as the president's eyes and ears. My own mission president took our role very seriously, and I considered it a sign of my commitment to missionary service that I would have the chance to work with him. All of this helped reinforce that outward and conscious commitment I had to do *everything* I could to obey.

And yet, on the other hand, way down inside my subconscious, buried under a thick layer of loyalty to Mormonism, I had a feeling that was a mix of boredom and frustration. I would not have been able to articulate it at the time, but I was starting to feel more and more that I was just performing a job – one that I never clocked out from. The daily, mundane grind of missionary service slowly began to take its toll. The conversation with a flirtatious girl my age was getting harder and harder to ignore. The desire to read something besides scriptures and a few approved books was increasing. I missed my classes at BYU-Idaho. I missed the regular visits to the temple I had before going to the mission. I missed my home community in Idaho, where the Mormon church was the norm, where there were no bottle-throwing, self-proclaimed Christians, and where everything was much simpler. I missed my family, whom I hadn't seen except in pictures in 18 months.

Although I now recognize this as the sort of normal, homesick reaction any 20-year-old would have had in my position, at the time, I didn't see it as such. To me, these were not the buried feelings of a young man under intense stress. They were a sign of weakness, failure, and giving in to the adversary. Satan was doing his part to tear me down, which meant that I had to redouble my efforts. When my mission president released me from my calling as an assistant and sent me back into the field as a standard missionary, I was internally deeply ashamed, thinking that my malaise had caused him to be disappointed. To make up for what I saw as defeat, I resolved that the last few months of my mission would be my most successful.

So, by the time that late-winter day arrived in 2005, when I had only a few months left, I was under massive psychological pressure – like a boiler about to explode. With very little time left, I felt that I had not accomplished what I knew I could accomplish, that what I had accomplished was no better than some middle management job, and that, with very little time left, I could not wait any longer. I was going to have to be more like Abraham: unflinching in the face of a harsh commandment and willing to do literally anything for Heavenly Father. It was now or never, and I could no longer just be the "small rules" following missionary. Only the Big Rule, to save Heavenly Father's children, really mattered.

The day had begun like most others. My companion and I were temporarily training a new missionary until he could be placed with an individual trainer. We got up, had breakfast, read our scriptures alone and together, planned and prayed, and headed out the door. Recently, our mission president had set a work goal for the entire mission; on select days ("Walk and Talk" days), we were to put away the cars and the bikes, and start walking the streets of our area, talking with every person we met about the gospel. When we came to a parking lot or a shopping center, we were to not let a single person get by without talking. When we came to a neighborhood, every door had to be knocked. Our mission president promised us that, if we followed the goal to the letter, the Lord would bless us with people who had open hearts and eager minds. On this day, my companions and I were read to Walk and Talk.

By this point in my mission, the reactions we got were not new. Every missionary interaction follows a similar pattern, assuming it gets passed the "I'm not interested" stage. It's true that each missionary has their favorite phrases to break the ice, things that catch people off guard: "Hey, would you like some good news today?" "Have you thought about Jesus today?" "How would you like to hear about something that will completely change your life?" But after these little personal touches start the conversation, the story is essentially the same. Start by setting a foundation of what a person already believes: is there a god, who is Jesus, what is the Bible, etc. Most individuals in Texas didn't require much effort to find some common ground. Next, use that foundation to raise harder questions: where were we before this life, what is it we're supposed to do here, how do we know that this or that church is true, what steps does god want us to take in this world, what is Heaven really going to be like, and (most importantly) how come god stopped sending prophets like Moses? These and similar questions are designed to find holes in their beliefs that only Mormonism could plug. If these questions prompted more dialogue, then it was time to tell the story of Mormonism – the one I recounted in the previous chapter. It was crucial to make it abundantly clear that the only reason Mormonism could be definitively true is because Joseph Smith was a prophet who got all this directly from the mouth of god. How could we prove it? *The Book of Mormon* is evidence that god spoke to Joseph; if this book is scripture, then everything else follows and Mormonism could be trusted. So…would you like to read this book? Aside from slight deviations depending on the person, this was always how the initial conversation went.

We walked and talked all morning. We took a break for lunch, gathered our strength, and worded the rest of the afternoon, making a large circle that would bring us back to our apartment in time to be at dinner at a member's house. By late afternoon, we were in a neighborhood knocking on doors as people came home from work and school. Some folks politely listened for a few minutes, ultimately sending us away, smiling to mask their annoyance. Most peopled didn't bother opening their doors or would only call through the eyehole, "Not interested!" The occasional few would listen and suggest we come back another time when they were less busy, knowing full well they would be conveniently not around when that later time came.

But there was one door that stood out to me not because of what the person on the other side did – but because of how I reacted. After a long day of walking, I was tired, and my outer walls of calm were starting to come down. Perhaps it was aching feet or the soreness in my legs that triggered it. Or maybe it was the fact that one of my companions – someone I had grown to admire greatly – would be leaving soon, further heightening my underlying sense of urgency. Or maybe, like the last snowflake that breaks the heavily iced tree, it was something imperceptible and unrelated. Whatever it was, when that Pentecostal preacher opened his door and smiled cunningly at the three haggard young men he saw standing there, I felt something in me give out.

The conversation started with pleasantries: why are you here, we have a message, what message is that, Mormonism, what could

Mormonism offer a Pentecostal preacher, the truth. We raised the hard questions, all of which he played along with, smiling widely the whole time. We told him the Mormon answers to those questions, and we told him that they are answers directly from god. We gave him the Joseph Smith story and ended with an offer of a *Book of Mormon* and free reading lessons to go with it. And then things took a hard left turn into confrontation. The preacher said something to the effect of, "Well, gentlemen, I have heard what you have to say, and I have heard plenty about Mormonism before this. And as I have preached to my own congregation, we must beware of 'wolves in sheep's clothing.' I feel it is my duty to call all three of you to repentance right here and now." He stepped out onto his porch, stood in front of us, and looked me in the eye (probably for no other reason than I was the tallest), and said, "You are a midwife of Satan. And hell is your destiny if you don't profess the name of the Lord Jesus."

Somewhere in me that 12-year-old boy from Idaho – the one who had fallen in love with Mormonism, who had given up his teen years and early adulthood for Mormonism, and who had been on a mission for almost two years to teach Mormonism – felt like he had been punched in the face. And the 20-year-old version of me was going to rectify that injury right here, right now. There had been other preachers before, other well-meaning individuals who had tried to do their own converting. Why it was this particular preacher hit the right button is hard to say. But in that moment, I felt the internal boiler explode.

I have not felt since and hope to never feel again the kind of burning, rage-fueled hatred for another person that I felt that day in early 2005. I didn't just want to prove this man wrong: I wanted him to never forget the time that Mormon missionary destroyed everything he held dear. Most of what followed was a blur of angry words. I told him what a pathetic, ridiculous religion his was, how drained of any substance it had. I demanded that he give me some proof for why he believed he could preach some evidence of authority from god. Oh, it's only a "calling" in your heart? Well, let me give you my authority – line of priesthood succession going from one hand to the next all the way to Joseph Smith who received it from the resurrected Jesus himself. And I had a book to prove it. Oh, you have a book, too? Oh, you think this or that verse helps you. Did you bother to read the verses before and after? *Can* you read, you drooling Southern chimp? How about a few verses you didn't bother to read, and which you now don't seem to have an answer for? How about we try my book now, a book that isn't full of the incoherent, sister-raping ramblings of the Iron Age morons that wrote your book? My book boasts of truth directly from the mouth of god to one man – a man that believed in a better world, a man that died penniless, a man that was butchered by the same ilk of this slimy charlatan that stands before me. This is an awfully nice house you have – how does it feel to know that you cheated a series of grieving grandmothers out of their husbands' pensions when they were desperate for Heaven? What did you tell them when they asked why they are here, where were they before, and where are they going? You didn't have those answers did you, or the most you had were vague statements of "Trust god" or "Just have faith." You call yourself a follower of Jesus? Where are the holes in the soles of your shoes, the bruises on your back from the paintball guns and the bottles? Where are the bags under your eyes from the daily, monotonous drudgery of getting a bunch of east Texas hicks to shut up for a few minutes and listen to someone other than themselves? Did you speak to your family today? I didn't, and haven't since Christmas. You condemn me? Well, while we're at it, let me promise you this, you benighted sophist, you washed up magician who peddles lies for his own bank account: when the Lord returns in all his glory and brings with him the saints that you whipped with your words, you will burn. Everything you love, all the people you hold dear, will melt before your eyes, and the clarion call of my god's trumpets will be the last thing you hear before you spend a thousand years in darkness.

Something to that effect. I'm not sure how much of his own thoughts he managed to get in, but the wry smile faded from his face, shifted to anger, dripped into confusion, and ended in fear of this fuming Mormon, who seemed to be hell bent on not leaving his porch. Multiple times he demanded we leave, trying to close the door behind him as I held it open with my body. It has become clear to him that this conversation was over, and all he wanted to do was see me leave. And I believe I had the energy to still be standing there to this day, like a Yellowstone geyser that hasn't shut off in decades, were it not for the companion that was leaving soon. His hand on my shoulder shook me out of my breakdown and brought me back to the moment. I turned and looked at him. What I saw was disappointment at what I had just demonstrated in front of a new missionary, our trainee – who was mostly standing there open-mouthed through the whole interaction. I stood in awkward silence as my companion apologized to the preacher and said we'd be on our way. As I shifted away from the door, it slammed in my face.

The walk home was a long, silent one. My companion didn't really have much to say except to explain to our trainee that what he had seen was not the kind of thing missionaries do. I tried to apologize to them both, and I offered to walk back and apologize to the preacher. But we pressed on. Soon, we were home, getting ready for dinner at a member's house. The daylight faded, our workday wound down, and we returned home to pray and plan our next day. Soon, that interaction faded into the past, nothing more than a note in a daily planner about what we had done on Walk and Talk Day.

I'm virtually certain that my companion would only vaguely remember that day, but I have never forgotten the moment I went full zealot.

2. Certainty, Opposition, and Control

I have more mission stories like this one, about myself and others. I have stories about holding other missionaries accountable, stories about vehemently debating theology, stories about long hunger fasts to increase my spirituality. I have stories where I helped other missionaries and members who were struggling with their faith by debunking "anti-Mormon" claims. I have no shortage of evidence of my zealotry and the steps I took to mask my internal frustration with myself and what I saw as my own failure to be the person Heavenly Father had promised I could be.

But I have shared this one because I think that it highlights a crucial distinction between zealotry and apatheism. As I explained in the previous chapter, zealotry has a specific meaning in the context of apatheism as *an attitude of intensity directed toward beliefs*. As I said, cult leaders or suicide bombers – people who go to extreme measures to express their religious beliefs – may share the same beliefs with other practitioners of their faiths and yet display those beliefs through a much more intense attitude. And by highlighting that intensity, I have shown that apatheism is the counterpoint to it: an attitude of indifference and reduced energy directed toward beliefs. Yet, a key feature I highlighted in my definition of zealotry is the exclusivity of the zealot's attitude. That aspect needs to be fully addressed here.

There are three features of zealotry that are tied to its exclusivity: The first is *certainty of belief*. A zealot's beliefs are not simply good ideas or one possible lens through which one can look at the world. True zealotry requires an attitude of certainty that the beliefs one has are correct. This can be obvious in how a zealot behaves; the men who flew airplanes into the World Trade Center on 9/11 conveyed to the world that they were certain they were doing Allah's will. But certainty of belief can be more subtle. It can be a disinterest in hearing counterpoints or consuming media that does not confirm the zealot's beliefs. It can be a preoccupation with beliefs, even to the point that those beliefs are the *sole* lens through which the zealot views the world. It can be an undeviating code of conduct that, at times, compels the zealot to behave in ways that can only be justified through the zealot's beliefs.

Whatever form it takes, certainty of belief is a fixed, immobility in a zealot's attitude.

The second feature of zealotry is the corollary of the certainty: *opposition to other beliefs and attitudes*. For the zealot, it is not enough to be convey certainty of beliefs through their behavior. A zealot also takes a defiant approach to beliefs and attitudes that are not theirs. A zealot sees the world in either/or: either my belief is right or yours is right, without the possibility of coexistence. And because the zealot is already certain, they see the world as one full of conflict with their beliefs. In their actions, zealots remove themselves from communities that differ from them. They arm themselves with evidence and justification for their own beliefs, and they are ready to share those points as often as possible. Indeed, a zealot is ready at a moment's notice to defend their ideas against opposing views.

But if those were the only features of zealotry then an awful lot of us would be zealots. Human beings tend to cling tenaciously to beliefs, even in the face of contradictory evidence or outside force. You can probably list a few of your own beliefs that fit this mold. In fact, an attitude of certainty might be a helpful mental mechanism that we possess to make sense of a sometimes-confusing world. Using heuristics – mental shortcuts – that are grounded in beliefs saves us an enormous amount of time and energy in the day to day. Rather than having to address our beliefs every waking moment, we can do the confirmatory work on the front end and never have to revisit it. Moreover, we naturally oppose those things that are unusual, different, or frightening to us. It is the mark of our evolved nature that we, like other living things, resist those things that might pose a danger to us. In matters of politics, economics, culture, relationships, and so forth, we are often opposed to those things that don't ring true to us. These two features on their own are not particularly earth-shattering; were it any other way, life would be pretty boring.

But that is why the third feature of zealotry is so important. Zealotry as I am defining it here also includes *a claim to the right to exercise power over the beliefs and attitudes of other people while demanding exemption for one's own beliefs and attitudes.* A zealot takes their certainty and their opposition one step further by domination. For a zealot, it is not enough that their beliefs and attitudes are theirs and other beliefs and attitudes are unpersuasive. A zealot cannot tolerate a world where different beliefs and attitudes exist. A zealot wants more zealots. The problems of the world and the chaos would be lessened if only there were more people like the zealot. The zealot then goes about working to make that vision a reality in whatever form of domination they can. This may be obvious domination: murder, destruction of property, true threats, or abuse. But it could also be in the form of active proselytizing, massive outreach campaigns, constant references to beliefs in social circles, broken friendships, and so forth. At the exact same time, the zealot contradictorily demands a special exemption from similar treatment. The zealot cannot tolerate the actions of competing zealots. They cry foul when another person comes knocking on their door to tell them they are wrong, but they are more than willing to do so themselves. They are fine with rules of conduct that are generally applicable to everyone else – drug laws, constraints on speech or press, lack of access to public resources, etc. – but demand that *they* be given exemption from those rules. After all, they are on the right side of the debate, so why should they be treated the same as others? At the most extreme, a zealot might display a type of persecution complex, believing that the world has conspired against their chosen beliefs and that a war is coming. For them, the wind is constantly blowing, and they feel like the last leaf on the tree.

It is that lack of reciprocity that is so crucial in this discussion. It is one thing to be certain of beliefs and to oppose counterpoints; it is quite another to claim the right to change or control other people while demanding special protection for oneself. Zealotry cuts to the heart of what we often think of as intolerant behavior. A tolerant person may not be pleased that others disagree, but they are willing to live in a world where everyone has the space to express that disagreement. A zealot cannot abide any of that. In their attitude with the world, they behave as a child who asks everyone else to share with them but refuses to do so in return.

Against this backdrop, it should be easy to see what makes an apatheist. If we accept my definition of zealotry, then someone who displays an attitude of indifference toward their religious beliefs and grace toward those of others has demonstrated the hallmark of apatheism. Where religious zealots intend on fashioning the world in their own image, the apatheist lives and lets live. Like the zealot, they may in fact be certain of their beliefs and they may oppose the beliefs and attitudes of others. They may be passionate and vocal in their own beliefs. But unlike zealots, they actively agree to live by a common set of rules that allow others the equal freedom to do the same. The zealot prioritizes their religious beliefs above all other principles. The apatheist expresses a commitment to respecting the human first and the beliefs second. And even if the apatheist has an attitude of willingness to share their beliefs, then they also have an attitude by which they're comfortable with the right of others to do so as well. In as simple terms as possible, apatheism is reciprocal indifference – the panacea to zealotry.

3. Apatheism for Individuals and Communities

This distinction between apatheism and zealotry on reciprocity grounds can be further extended along the lines of a feature that raised in my outline in the first chapter. As I indicated in that outline, apatheism can be considered both a private attitude as well as a public-facing one. Because it is ultimately the way in which one positions themselves toward their beliefs and displays them to the world, apatheism has both internal and external effects on us and others. Indeed, it is its reciprocity that gives it both a personal and communal flavor.

The idea of behavioral concepts having private/public components is not a new concept. Within ethics and political philosophy, there has regularly been recognition that concepts like "the good," "the just," or "the right" have both individual definitions as well as definitions that are shared by a broader community, including a nation. For example, much of Enlightenment political philosophy wrestled with how morality has both a virtuous element ("I should be a good person") as well as a legal element ("A society should be just society"). In fact, this is often a feature of our own discourse in the United States. Many of the things we do on a day-to-day basis are not grounded in public law: holding a door open for a person, donating money to a charity or a person in need, being honest with coworkers, keeping promises to others, etc. At the same time, there is an elaborate and complex system of public rules that preserve order and help minimize conflicts among us.

Our liberal form of government in the United States and in many developed nations[31] often assumes that these two aspects are essential to our society. Consider, for example, the Free Speech Clause of the First Amendment and the case law that has interpreted it. On the one hand, the clause protects our right to have our own ideas, to develop them, and to express them. The government – whether federal or State – cannot force you to think certain ideas or prevent you from expressing those ideas based on their content. For the most part, the government operates on the idea that individuals are in the best position to decide what is good for them. The term "marketplace of ideas" is often overused and applied inconsistently, but at a basic level, it stands for the idea that society is better off when the government generally maintains neutrality on ideas. Given the choice between constraints on thoughts and expression versus liberty to debate and criticize, our society embraces the latter as the better way to identify truth and protect individuals. In a nutshell, letting you be an autonomous agent of your own ideas is going to produce better

---

[31] I am using liberal in its philosophical sense, not its political sense. By "liberal," I don't mean the Democratic party or the progressive left wing of politics. Rather, I mean the political theory of liberalism, in its broadest sense. It is beyond the scope of this book to explain what philosophical liberalism is, but about five minutes of online research should clear it up.

results than some outside force dictating your own ideas. Let's call this concept *your theory of the good life*.

On the other hand, the Free Speech Clause also holds that we, acting through our government, have the right – even the duty – to referee this so-called marketplace to maintain its freedom. While the clause prevents constraints on *content*, it does permit constraints on behavior that would silence, abuse, or destroy the freedom of others to hold their own ideas. The minute that you exercise your freedom to take away someone else's freedom, we, collectively, can use our political will to stop you from doing so or rectify the harm you have caused. A great example of this is speech that incites crime. Under this line of cases, a speaker can be punished for expressing ideas that incite people to commit unlawful conduct, provided that there is an intent by the speaker to do so and that there is an imminent connection between the speech and the unlawful behavior.[32] What we're punishing here is not necessarily ideas – as bad as they may be, but we're punishing the fact that those ideas have led to the abuse of other people or their property. The intent of this aspect of government is to ensure that people *really do* have the freedom to develop their own ideas and not risk being threatened by speakers who would deprive them of their freedom to do so by threats or criminal behavior. Let's call this concept *our theory of the just society*.

This tension between the individual's private theory of the good life versus the community's theory of the just society is the

---

[32] This line of cases is often referred to as the "incitement cases," the most important of which is the *Brandenburg* case from 1969. There are an endless amount of resources for learning about this topic, and I encourage you to do so.

heart and soul of contemporary politics; finding some equilibrium between these two theories is quite literally the point of the "American project" from its inception. Pick any contemporary problem: tax policy, climate change, social justice, identity politics, education, policing. At its core, that problem will involve a discussion of how much space should be given for individuals to dictate their own lives versus how much power the community must constrain people from violating equal freedom. Wrapped up in this conversation is the question of how much an individual is exempt from the constraining power of their community. To what degree can a person follow the dictates of their own theory of the good without running afoul of community freedom? And how much are they willing to afford their fellow community members that same freedom?

In this religious context, apatheism is much more consistent than zealotry with this theory of good vs. just approach to the civil society. On the one hand, private apatheism is a component of an individual's theory of the good life. Private apatheism is an attitude of indifference toward prioritizing one belief over another in one's personal life and immediate social circle. It is the kind of apatheism that individuals display in how they allocate their own time and resources. Rather than let religion become the dominating authority over every decision one makes, apatheism includes it as one of many components to a theory of the good life. Privately, an apatheistic person makes their life decisions based on disparate factors, none of which is necessarily offset by their beliefs about the existence of non-existence of god. Moreover, an apatheist interacts with their family, friends, coworkers, and immediate community members based on multiple sources of belief – not just religious ones. They expect similar treatment in return. Even if their theory of ethical behavior may take different forms, the apatheist nevertheless includes an attitude of religious indifference in their theory of the good life.

Public apatheism is the same attitude that an individual displays, but it is incorporated into a community's theory of a just society. It is that attitude that groups and states promote in their communal relationships: citizens, corporations, governments, and so forth. An apatheistic community embraces the notion that a just society is one that affords – and takes *seriously* – multiple religious beliefs' equal freedom for development and expression. The apatheistic community does not prefer one set of religious beliefs over another or religious belief over irreligion, does not prioritize resources for religious belief, and does not punish or otherwise pressure those who do not endorse religious belief. In matters of religious *content*, the apatheistic community is indifferent – the content-neutral corollary of Free Speech. This same community, however, will step in when this principle of equal freedom is threatened by individuals or small groups. When such an individual or group within the community tries to dominate non-believers, deprive others of their freedom, or demand special exemptions from equal freedom based on their religious beliefs, then the community reserves the right to correct or refuse to accommodate them. In a nutshell, the community acts as umpire to prevent the very freedom individuals demand from being diminished.

4. The Gulf Between Apatheism and Zealotry

The distinction I have drawn between zealotry and apatheism – namely, the presence of reciprocity – is very much the lynchpin of private and public apatheism. In theory, it is not any more complicated than affording others the same rights that you claim for yourself. Zealotry as I have defined it is the assertion that one has a right or power over another person/group/community to constrain beliefs to fit one's own definition of good. But what makes that space between zealotry and apatheism so large – what creates the awful gulf between them – is the level of proof that zealotry would require. It is difficult to imagine a scenario in which an individual or community could plausibly claim they have the right of dominion over others that they claim to have.

The amount of proof necessary would be daunting. A person would first have to show that he or she is somehow superior to or at least so different from others that they are exceptional – an outlier from the rest of us. Next, that person would have to show that this exceptionalism has some connection to their beliefs – that their religious beliefs are either what make them exceptional or that those beliefs are an expression of their exceptionalism. Moreover, they would then have to show how others who *also* claim this right of exceptionalism are wrong in their beliefs. They would have to appeal to some objective standard that would satisfy the rest of us in a conflict between two people who claim exceptionalism. Finally, and most importantly, even after proving all of that, the exceptional person would have to show that it would be in the best interests of others to yield to this exceptionalism and modify their religious beliefs to fit the exceptional person's standard.

Zealots deny reciprocity under the assumption that they have met all these burdens of proof – or at least that they are messengers for someone who has. But, in actuality, the sheer magnitude of the proof required to demonstrate this level of certainty is likely part of the reason why many zealot religions depend on founding stories, in which the authoritative person does not claim to be exceptional but has some direct connection to someone who is – like a god or prophet. Those beliefs are all well and good on their own; if a person chooses to live under the assumption that they are so special that norms, customs, rules, and laws don't apply to them, then so be it. But it's a massive leap in logic to then claim that this justifies interference with others' beliefs or that the rest of us should abandon our beliefs for some other set. Apatheism is the attitude that rejects this certainty-based-interference. No matter the degree of one's apatheism, it is a fundamental characteristic of apatheism that one denies this right to authoritative exceptionalism in matters of religious belief and demands that others treat one another with the same reciprocity.

If all this abstract talk of theory is too dry, then allow me to put it in concrete terms. In the previous chapter, I distinguished apatheism and zealotry in terms of intensity. In that chapter, I demonstrated that my 12-year-old self transitioned to zealotry as I intensely committed to my Mormon beliefs. Before that moment, Mormonism was one characteristic of my childhood – one of many interests and identities I was already beginning to cultivate on into adolescence and adulthood. But from that moment, the temperature on my attitude toward my Mormon beliefs ratcheted up significantly. I adopted from then on the first feature of zealotry: an attitude of intensity to my beliefs.

In this chapter, I have further distinguished the concepts in terms of reciprocity. As my story in this chapter highlights, my 20-year-old missionary self, steeped in Mormonism, adopted the second feature of zealotry: lack of reciprocity. As I hope that story conveys, I was more than willing to control the lives of others. That preacher was going to do what other non-Mormon preachers had done to me and my companions countless times before: he was going to share his own zealotry. In the past, I might have brushed it aside or respectfully debated religious points with him. Most likely, it would have ended with me simply saying the preacher had his chance to accept the true gospel and it was his loss. But my zealot intensity had grown and grown to that point, and it spilled over into controlling the life of another person. I had shown up at his house just after he came home from work, and on terms not of his choosing. He had not asked me to come and explain to him why his religion was false. His annoyance and his own desire to protect his beliefs drove him to say what he had said. Maybe he had intended to provoke me or maybe he had simply wanted to get me off his porch so he could have dinner. Yet, there I was, attacking him, dumping out all the inner frustration with myself that I had kept bottled up. I hated him, and I wanted to take away something from him for what I believed was his own good. And I was not at all willing to grant him any similar concessions. Only *I* was in charge of that moment – not him.

But what is perhaps hardest about this story is not that it happened, but that I liked it. As ashamed as I was, I felt in that moment that I had followed through on the logical conclusion of my zealotry. I have similar stories where this sort of thing happened to myself or to other missionaries around me. As much as the daily grind had been drudgery, let's be honest: I delighted in enforcing mission rules, in knocking on the doors of non-Mormons, in teaching the Mormon gospel, and in passionately declaring my beliefs. I also had no problem claiming that as a unique right for myself and for Mormonism generally. I could not imagine sitting through someone else's explanation of their faith, unless it was to find common ground that I could use to spread my own faith. I gave myself grace and mercy to grow as a Mormon teenager and then as a Mormon missionary, while at the same time expecting others to have already accomplished their growth or at least be willing to let me control their growth. When I look back on that event with that preacher, I see a version of myself that could not tolerate difference.

Most profound of all is the fact that I believed that I was very much on the side of certainty and truth. That preacher was wrong, I was right – what more needed to be said? I had been taught a simple reality from birth: that Mormonism is not just a new way of looking at the world, but the *only* way of looking at the world if one wanted to please Heavenly Father. We had all agreed in the Preexistence that we would come here, get physical bodies, and find our way back "home." Heavenly Father had promised that he would send messengers to help us find that straight and narrow path that led home. He had sent prophets before; he could send them again. And he did, when he appeared to Joseph Smith in a grove of trees and told him no other religion was true or had the authority to teach people. God's children needed Joseph and Joseph needed helpers. I had the privilege to be one of them. And *The Book of Mormon*, the feelings in my heart, and the constant repetition of the Mormon gospel was all the proof anyone would need to see my certainty. It wasn't *me* that was changing people's beliefs; I was just a conduit through which Heavenly Father could act. If they felt pressured, they could take it up with him. I was just doing my part so that "the blood and sins of this generation" would not be on *my* hands when Jesus returned to say the work was done. If at times I went a little overboard and made people like my admirable companion uncomfortable, well, then so be it. I wanted Jesus to someday hug me and say, "Well done, thou good and faithful servant."

Rest assured, too, that this sort of attitude is part and parcel of being a Mormon. I didn't invent this attitude out of thin air; it was modeled for me. Mormonism *is* intense, it *does* claim to be exceptional, it *does* interfere in the lives of others, and it *does* refuse other religions any reciprocity on that front. If Mormonism abandoned all of that, it would deny the very story it told to the world: that we're here to be tested and tried to see if we will make it back to Heavenly Father. It's the reason the Mormon church spends millions annually in public relations and marketing campaigns, why it spends millions more on temples and meetinghouses, and why it prints millions of copies of *The Book of Mormon* to give away for free. It's the reason why a Mormon would be mortified and deeply offended if someone were to show up at their door to condemn them. It's the reason the Mormon church and its members constantly claim to be persecuted when any critical attention is directed their way. It's the reason it fights tooth and nail in court proceedings to control its own narrative. It's the reason that Mormons make lists of their neighbors that they can share the gospel with and send the missionaries to. It's the reason why Mormons can't imagine anyone leaving the faith and why it is so bureaucratically difficult to no longer be Mormon. It's the reason why even now, years later and after having repeatedly asked to be left alone, ex-Mormons like me are contacted by missionaries or local leaders to convince us to come back. It's the reason why I have had friends who no longer speak to me, simply because I am no longer a Mormon. It's the reason why family members will continually bring up Mormonism, send letters and texts, visit, make phone calls, etc., digging into the life of an ex-Mormon. And it's the reason why this book will almost certainly be branded "anti-Mormon literature" by some. Because Mormonism, like so many other organized faiths, is inherently zealot.

As I said at the beginning of this book, I am sharing my own experience with my past faith to better explain the theoretical concepts that underlie zealotry and apatheism. But it really should not be that hard to see how these same concepts are present all over the world today in one form or another. The case of Matthew Coleman is an intentionally stark case study of intense attitude toward beliefs, claims of exceptionalism, denial of reciprocity, and assertions that one can interfere in the lives of others – by putting spear holes through the chests of one's own children who are under the age of five. Pick a recent, violent act done in the name of religion, and I can guarantee that you will find the hallmarks of zealotry surrounding it. Go even deeper. Look for all the religious examples of dominance and authority that are shoved on children or the weak, the threats of what will happen if someone doesn't obey or leaves a religion, the political demands of some religious people to change laws to fit their beliefs or to give themselves exemptions to the rules by which the rest of us live. Look for all those religions who expect tithing and donations to fund their efforts, and they pay their ministry exorbitant salaries or fight governments tooth and nail against paying taxes. And when you're done doing that, scan the world for all the people who shrug at the vocal, hysterical minority that would work its will on all of us. The truly powerful in the face of zealots are those who can stand on their own porch, look a rage-filled Mormon missionary or arrogant Pentecostal preacher dead in the eye, and say, "I don't care."

So much for theory. Up until now we've examined some broad concepts about apatheism to distinguish it from its zealot counterpart. But the conversation thus far has only focused on that fundamental difference. Unfortunately, as is often the case, the practice of things like reciprocity and tolerance is often harder than theory makes them sound. To move the conversation forward, in the next chapter I will discuss the three basic attitudes of an apatheist "to get down to brass tacks." As that discussion will hopefully show, the attitude of an apatheist – like the religious beliefs to which they are directed – is a spectrum with significant variability. As I will show, an apatheistic attitude does not have to be all or nothing; rather, such an attitude can be directed to at least three types of religious beliefs. After exploring that facet of apatheism, my final chapter will discuss what is at stake for us in the apatheist/zealot distinction. When framed in the contemporary social context, I think it will be easier to see how apatheism – and, by extension, intensity-drained reciprocity – is not only very possible, but something many people already display.

The "Big Three" Attitudes

The beauty of religious mania is that it has the power to explain everything. Once God (or Satan) is accepted as the first cause of everything which happens in the mortal world, nothing is left to chance…or change…To the true religious maniac, it's all on purpose.
– Stephen King

1. Oh, God…Where Art Thou?

In the summer of 2016, the year I turned 32, I sat in a therapist's office, crying harder than I ever had in my adult life. I had been with her for almost an hour, and something she had asked me had prompted this sobbing. It was the sort of crying that comes from deep down inside you, the way you cry as a child when you feel abandoned and terrified when you cannot find you parent. It was simultaneously healing and bitterly painful; I had needed to do this for years, but it involved me tearing out a part of myself that I loved for so long, raising a knife to it, and watching it writhe and die. I had ascended the psychological mount for this very purpose, but that rational reality did not make it any easier.

My 20s had been a whirlwind of change. I returned home from my mission in August 2005 and immediately picked up my college career right where I had left off. Life as a returned missionary ("RM") was wonderful; I had "passed the test" so to speak and had come out the other side as a young man with newfound worth in the eyes of my community. I was no longer following such a rigid schedule with such a high-stakes purpose. The task that was now laid before me was simple: get an education, live the gospel I had taught on my mission and – above all – get married. About three weeks after I came home, I returned to BYU-Idaho and jumped into that task with both feet. I declared a major in English and a minor in philosophy, fell in love with literature and Christian theology, and found a cohort of fellow young Mormons at BYU-Idaho that shared my worldview. I got a job at the campus NPR affiliate, ultimately producing my own jazz show. I wrestled with what I wanted to do as a career. Should I do what my parents had done and become a teacher? I loved being a student and enjoyed every chance I got to teach. Was a career in academia right for me? On the other hand, I had seen how difficult it was for my parents, as public-school teachers, to make ends meet. I didn't want to be in the position someday of having to worry endlessly about money; that would distract from my bigger spiritual goals. I resolved that I would table that decision until I was married and instead focus on maintaining the high GPA, I needed for the merit scholarship I had received when I was a pre-mission freshman.

But none of that was as important to me as finding an "eternal companion" with whom I could start a family. Mormon doctrine, as I explained in an earlier chapter, teaches that returning home to Heavenly Father requires both significant faith and daily gospel living but saving ordinances as a well. It is worth explaining that feature in more detail to fully understand what is in the mind of a Mormon in their early 20s. Without the priesthood authority of the Mormon church, as delegated to Joseph Smith by Jesus Christ, even the most righteous could not be saved. God's house is a house of order, and the priesthood ordinances were essential to being able to get back into god's presence, to "pass the angels who stand as sentinels" guarding the way to the Celestial Kingdom. These ordinances were expressions of a covenant with Heavenly Father – binding agreement that, in exchange for his blessings, the recipient would commit to certain commandments. So, starting at age eight, every Mormon obtains these ordinances: baptism for the remission of sins and the gift of the Holy Ghost (age 8), ordination into the Aaronic and Melchizedek priesthoods for young men, weekly partaking of the sacrament (throughout life after baptism), initiatory and endowment in the temple (pre-mission or pre-marriage), and sealing, or marriage, in the temple. Mormons are taught that everything aims toward the temple and to an eternal marriage in which a person is "sealed" to their spouse for "time and all eternity." The temple ordinances, including marriage, are treated as the pinnacle of sacredness because of their exalting quality. These do not simply *save* you from sin and death, but they prepare you to obtain the higher blessings of the Celestial Kingdom and the kind of life that Heavenly Father lives. Just as I was taught as a teenager that nothing could be more important than my preparing for a mission, I was taught in my late-teens and early 20s that nothing could be more important than a temple marriage.

So, I made myself a goal: I would find and marry someone as soon as possible so that I could get on with a dedicated Mormon life and start raising good Mormon children. As a lawyer, I figured I would have ample ability to provide for a family, such that my wife wouldn't have to work and could nurture our children. Prior to my mission, I had been dating a girl that I thought at the time would be the person I would marry, but my life had changed significantly as a missionary. Instead, I dated as often as I could, usually in an urgent, desperate sort of way. Looking back, I recognize with some embarrassment that I was kind of a lot and what the Gen Z population would call "thirsty." One woman I dated informed me after a couple of months that she was going on a mission, prompting me to call off the relationship; I just couldn't wait the 18 months she would be a missionary.

It was in between the summer of my sophomore year that I found the person I most needed in my life; if you had sat me down that summer, explained all that I was going to face over the next two decades, and told me that the person I would meet that summer would be the *only* person who could see me through it, I would not have even had the framework to understand the magnitude of what you were saying. When Emily Watson walked into my life one summer day in 2006, there was suddenly a lighthouse shining in the dark storms on my horizon that I had not yet even sensed were brewing. To say that things happened quickly with Emily and me would be an understatement. We met in early summer, by August we were engaged, and by Christmas we were married. We often joke that that schedule of events had a little help from the Mormon ban on premarital sex. But all these years later,

I see something more at work: two people who unconsciously recognized that they needed one another to hold on to when everything else came crumbling down.

At the age of 20 and 22, respectively, Emily and I started 2007 as a newly married couple living in abject poverty. Our first apartment was a dimly lit hovel that we did our best to turn into a home. During the school year, we scrapped by on whatever money the two of us could make as students, while during the summer, we worked endless hours to save enough for the coming year's rent. After we graduated, we moved to Logan, Utah, where I spent a year teaching English at a public high school and where Emily worked as a graphic designer for a local small business. Although we were making more than we ever had, we knew it was temporary. When I met Emily, I realized that my future *must* include financial security, that being a good husband meant providing for the family I wanted. So, I had decided that, given the choice between academia and law, there was no contest: I would need to choose the latter as only it would give me the confidence that I was fulfilling my priesthood covenants.

That fall, simultaneously as the worst recession in a generation was just starting to rumble, I began applying to law schools, completely oblivious to what I was getting myself into. Emily, the faithful Mormon wife, supported me in that decision. When the admissions decisions rolled in, I went with the best option I believed I had, to start law school in the fall of 2009 at George Washington University Law School in Washington, DC. When summer came and the first day of law school was only a few weeks away, we packed our few belongings into a moving truck, loaded our aging Ford Taurus onto a trailer, and waved goodbye to family as we headed east.

I have worked hard in this book to root my theory of apatheism in my own experience as a Mormon turned apatheist. In doing so, I hope that my ideas have taken on some salience. If that is the case, then I need to draw a heavy, bold line under this moment in August 2009, when Emily and I drove eastward over the Rocky Mountains on I-80. It wasn't just an interesting turning point; it was a plot development of Biblical proportions: Adam and his wife leaving the Garden, eastward in Eden. I wasn't just leaving my home of 25 years; I was exiting the Mormon corridor of the Wasatch Front and blissfully unaware that nothing was *ever* going to be the same after that. I think back on that three-day journey across the country and see a young man who had only been out of Idaho and Utah for the occasional family vacation or for a mission. I see two people who had been married less than three years, who had no preparation for the unknown they were about to step into. I remember a moving van full of a cacophony of excitement, fear, ambition, and hope, mixed in with the smell of beef jerky and the sounds of every classic rock station from Utah to Virginia. I guess every young couple has their moments – this was ours.

I also cannot stress what a shock to my system Washington, DC, was. As a boy who had spent most of his life in rural Idaho, the "big city" was exciting and terrifying all at once. I had *never* been around so many people who were different from me: people of every race and ethnicity, of every gender identity, of every professional background, of every religion. In my law school classes,

I sat among people who came from monied, Ivy League backgrounds and people who, like me, had "gotten out" of their small hometowns. I met my first openly gay person, my first true feminist, my first Muslim, my first atheist. My two best friends in law school were a couple of Jewish guys who, like me, were on the older end of the law school spectrum. I was immediately hit with a flood of new ideas and beliefs that I had not encountered anywhere before in my life or had only barely read about. When Emily and I commuted into the city from Alexandria, VA, sometimes by bus and Metro and sometimes by car, we were surrounded by a level of difference that was as stark as the level of sameness we had just left. Quite literally, we had dived into the deep end.

It did not take long for this new world to begin changing us in different ways. There were the practical changes, like career goals and family planning. Emily and I had already agreed that we would put kids on hold until we felt we were more financially secure and less transient; the last thing we wanted was to bring a child into our insecurity. We were living off my student loans (which were rapidly adding up) and Emily's income as a graphic designer and then as a department administrator at my school. Emily had also decided that she too needed a graduate education to meet her own career goals, and we had started to moderate our belief in the "male provider, female nurturer" pattern we had been taught in church; after all, there were plenty of good Mormon women we were starting to encounter, who were working mothers. That meant that I needed to make law school count, that to pay back my debts I needed that coveted high-paying attorney job that everyone wanted. We both recognized that DC was where we were going to be for our immediate future.

But the changes were not just external; they were internal as well. I had believed all my life that there was one way to live, that there was one truth that would save people, and that there was one true moral code that people should follow if they wanted to be happy. God's children were scattered over the whole earth and, if they wanted to come home, they would have to embrace that reality. Although I was raised in a comparatively open-minded home, my broader community had taught me that things were safer in Mormondom, that I was lucky to be born in the place where I had grown up. The world – Babylon – was full of wickedness, temptation, and evil; it was ruled by Satan, who wanted to tear you down as part of his eternal effort to thwart Heavenly Father's plan of happiness. But in Mormondom – Zion – was the plain and simple gospel, goodness, and truth; its ruler was Jesus Christ, who would come off the victor in that conflict and redeem all those children who wanted to be redeemed.

And yet...everywhere I looked in DC there were good people – not just in the sense that they were "good people who were confused and needed a dose of truth," but really, truly *good* people. Sure, there was plenty about DC that was troubling and violent; you can't live in the Balt-Wash area and not encounter your fair share of Hobbes' state of nature. But I met an overwhelmingly large group of people who had their own moral code or who had come from cultures starkly different from my own, and yet they were as good as I was if not better. The lack of Mormonism in their life didn't seem to have any effect whatsoever on how they behaved. Early on, I tried to share and defend Mormonism with some of them, much like I had been taught to do as a missionary and encouraged to do as a church member. But over time I felt less and less of a need to do so – not because I was ashamed of my faith but because it seemed so unnecessary. I had been taught that Heavenly Father was a god of love, and here were many of his children who seemed to be doing quite well without my intervention. Whatever saving ordinances I could offer them seemed superfluous. Although I still proudly shared my faith when asked about it, the old urgency of my teens was melting away in the heat of camaraderie. Before, "those people out there" needed saving, beyond the walls of the Rocky Mountains; now that I was here, among "those people," it was hard to see what all the fear had been about. In fact, it started to feel arrogant and out of harmony.

Life soon got very busy. Against all odds, I managed to secure a junior associate position at a large, K Street law firm in DC. I graduated in spring 2012, and we moved to Maryland, halfway between Baltimore and DC. The plan was for Emily to start her MFA in Baltimore, while I commuted into the city start in October of that year, after I took and passed the Bar Exam. Although the last six years of our marriage had been financially and practically challenging, I chalked up these developments to our faithfulness. We were active in our ward and stake, we paid our tithing religiously, we prayed and fasted and obeyed all the commandments to the best of our ability, and when we screwed up, we repented.

That last one was especially crucial to me; every word, deed, and thought was an opportunity to beg god for forgiveness. As full as DC was with good people, it was still, after all, Babylon, and any chink in my spiritual armor could prove fatal. I still have saved, somewhere in my files, a spreadsheet I made during this time where I would track my daily worthiness – what sins I had committed that day and what I had done to overcome them. I covered myself in shame and guilt like sackcloth and ashes knowing that I was killing off the "natural man." In exchange for this constant psychological vigilance, Heavenly Father was blessing me so much: a good job, a good salary, a happy marriage. Emily and I were even called to be workers in the DC temple – a fact that proved undeniably to me that we were on the right path. The psychological exhaustion I felt mounting inside my brain was a small price to pay for acceptance by Heavenly Father. Life was going to be hard, but like Abraham, I would offer up whatever god needed if it meant I could be loved by him.

***

I cannot pinpoint the exact moment things began to fall apart. I do know that it was somewhere around 2013-2014, when a small brushfire started a slow burn in my spiritual life. There were a lot of factors that combined during this season to foment the change that was coming. First and most obvious was my career was not panning out at all in the way I had imagined. I had come to law school with zero preparation or support – I had no lawyers in my family, no prelaw advisor, and no mentor that could help me navigate the decision I had made to go to law school. I had decided on law because I needed a good income; good Mormon boys become good Mormon husbands, and good Mormon husbands provide for and protect their families. Law, with its emphasis on advocacy and debate, seemed like the logical career choice for me. I had fought tooth and nail in law school for the highest paid position that I could get and only squeaked by on what I thought was the tender mercies of the Lord. But the job I had coveted and thought would be the ticket to being that good Mormon husband was turning out to be the absolute worst career choice I could have made. The salary was nice enough, but large portions of it were going to student loans and 10% of it was going to the Mormon church in the form of tithing (about $17,000/year). In the three years I worked at my firm, I took one vacation and answered emails most of the time. My commute was at minimum an hour one way, and after spending 12-14 hours at the firm, I would commute home and work some more, often until 1:00-2:00 in the morning. I was at my computer constantly. Meanwhile, Emily kept her own schedule, heading the opposite direction to Baltimore. We hardly saw one another anymore, and when we did, that time was punctuated by me responding to an urgent email from the dozen or so bosses I had. Other people in the firm seemed to be thriving in this environment. But I was only growing to hate it.

And in addition to the malaise settling over my career, I was in the early stages of a nervous breakdown. At the same time that I was working long hours as an attorney, I was trying to be an active, committed Mormon. I was still trying to maintain the level of commitment I had always had to the church, and I was still trying my hardest to root out all evil from my life. That was getting harder and harder to do. When I snapped and lashed out in anger, I hated myself for it. When I let my mind wander to dark thoughts, I felt crippling shame and guilt. When I felt the need to lie or manipulate in my professional and personal life, I believed I was giving in to the natural man inside me. In my teens, I had obsessive compulsive tendencies – checking doors and windows at night to make sure they're locked, flipping light switches, washing my hands, not touching dirty surfaces. But as my mental need for cleanliness increased, so too did my OCD; there were times, during this season, where it would take me over an hour to get to bed because I followed an aggressive cycle of checking – constant checking.

I felt like an utter failure on every level. I was a bad husband, who hated his job and did the bare minimum to provide. I wasn't nurturing a climate of peace in my home and was dedicating almost no time to my relationship with Emily. I had yet to be a father – a fact that made me enormously guilty. Emily and I had tried multiple times to have a child, but for whatever reason, it never quite worked, so we would give up for a time. That fact made me feel like I had offended Heavenly Father, that I was not yet worthy to be a good dad to a child, no matter how desperately I wanted to be one. I was a bad son and sibling; I rarely saw my family, as we were separated by thousands of miles and conflicting schedules. I was a bad friend, who had lost touch with all those childhood and mission friends I had grown to love over the years. Worst of all, my program for purging sin from my life was floundering: every day I was filled with depressing thoughts and angry emotions, frustrated that nothing I did seemed to improve my spirituality. It had been years since the sweet peace of my mission; what I had now was chaos and frustration. Outwardly, I was a good Mormon man; inwardly, I was a raging ball of shame. Whoever might have hated me at the time couldn't even come close to how much I hated myself. My lowest point was on a winter day in 2014 when I had the distinct thought of jumping in front of the commuter trains that rushed through the station where I lived in Maryland. Standing inches from the edge of the platform, I had the very real thought to jump the three feet as I saw the train coming in the distance and just end it all.

While all of this was going on, events in the Mormon church were getting harder and harder to reconcile. Emily was the first of the two of us to start asking questions: Why were women not allowed to hold the priesthood? Why was it the case that a sacrament meeting at church could proceed without a single woman in the room but couldn't even start without at least one man present? Why was it the case that she, as a female temple worker, would have to leave her calling if she had a child but her husband would not? Why was it wrong to talk about a Heavenly Mother, when it was clear that Mormon doctrine was clear that she existed? Why was the Mormon church spending millions in lobbying and court cases to fight against LGBTQ rights? Why was the Mormon church spending similar dollars in investments and land holdings that didn't seem to be doing much to benefit the general membership? Why was it that women, like Kate Kelly and John Dehlin,[33] were being publicly excommunicated for even asking

---

[33] If you have not familiarized yourself with Kate Kelly and John Dehlin, I encourage you to do so. Their stories are readily available with some googling.

these legitimate questions out loud? Granted, Emily too was still very much a committed Mormon, albeit one who wished the Mormon church would change some of its less egalitarian policies. But when Emily shared her own views at the Kelly's excommunication vigil, I could feel a change coming in our lives. At home, our conversations were turning more and more to what our future was going to look like together.

***

What followed was a difficult season of cognitive dissonance for me between 2014 and the beginning of 2016. Those two years were in stark contrast to the two years I had spent as a Mormon missionary. On a professional level and at Emily's urging, I had decided to change careers – a decision that had required some brutal soul searching. I had gone to law school in the hope of supporting my family; what I had sacrificed in the offing was any sense of personal accomplishment or self-worth. I enjoyed studying the law as an academic process, but I hated being a lawyer and hated the lifestyle it was thrusting on me. I could not envision the next 40-50 years of my life defending clients who were out to extract every dollar and pound of flesh they could from others. It was clear to me that, between law and academia, I had chosen poorly (another failure!) and now, before a child was brought into all of this, I needed to rectify that choice.

In 2015, I started a PhD at University of California-Davis, studying political philosophy. The breath of fresh air that decision brought into my life was liberating. I was out of the DC rat race, living in one of the most beautiful places in the world, and getting back to the books and ideas I had loved as an undergrad and a law student. My advisor, Bob Taylor, a man for whom I have the highest admiration, took a stressed-out lawyer, and molded him. During my study as a political theorist, a field of study that focuses on what is just and right for societies, I realized that there are rational arguments for a good world that don't depend on one's religion. I also realized that the world in which we live is profoundly diverse, that human beings should have the freedom to pursue whatever goals they choose, and that society should give them the space to work through that. If the endless religious wars of the past were to be avoided in the future, a just society needs to give people the right to believe what they wish without permitting violence and abuse to others in the name of god. That philosophically liberal realization was a powerful force in my life.

At the same time, I was going through these professional changes, I had become much more introspective about my beliefs, which inevitably led to cognitive dissonance. If Emily had started the process of thinking critically about Mormon beliefs, I exploded it. On one level, I still strongly believed that Mormonism was the truth. I believed Heavenly Father loved his children and had prepared a great plan for them to return home and be like him, with Jesus at the center of the plan. I believed we had been in the presence of Heavenly Father before we were born here and that this plan was taught to us, that we accepted it, and that there were some, like Lucifer, who rejected it to their destruction. I believed that Heavenly Father made the world and morality to test us – to put us in simulation – to see whether we would be worthy of exaltation. I believed that the Mormon church was the messenger of this plan to the world and that, although I was lucky to have been born a Mormon, I had a duty to share this truth with everyone. I believed that one day we would be judged for what we believed and did in this testing ground and that our eternal future depending on *everything* we did in life. So, on the one hand, the 12-year-old boy and the Mormon missionary I had been were still very much alive and well.

But on the other hand, my brain contained other, competing thoughts that I had difficulty reconciling with my faith. There were lots of historical and cultural issues that I worked through: the manner of Joseph Smith's translation of *The Book of Mormon*; the significant overlaps between that book and other books that Joseph would have had available to him; Joseph's polygamous (and at times, pedophilic) relationships; the overlap between the temple ordinances and the Masonic rituals of Joseph's day; the questionable origin of other writings Joseph said he translated from ancient texts, such as the *Book of Abraham*; and the Mormon church's many policies that seemed at odds with its stated goal of being Heavenly Father's kingdom on earth (*e.g.*, a racial ban on priesthood for Black men until 1978, a continuing gender ban against women holding the priesthood, the tight theocratic grip the church holds over regional politics in Utah, *etc.*). But none of these were faith-breaking for me; I found plenty of apologetic reasons to dismiss these seeming problems. At the end of the day, those questions were resolved with the reality that history is always messy, and no organization is perfect. As I often explain to anyone who asks, I did not leave Mormonism because of its messy origin or imperfections.

No, the questions that kept me up at night were more fundamental, more doctrinal. They cut to the heart of the Mormon belief system. For instance, suppose such a plan of salvation *did* exist and that Heavenly Father had created it with our final destination in mind. To what purpose? Sure, this plan would lead to our salvation and exaltation, but to what end? Mormonism had taught me that it and it alone had the *only* answers to the three big questions: where we came from, why we're here, and where we're going. But did the Mormon plan of salvation really have those answers?

To put my thinking in clear terms, think through the following analogy with me: Suppose that you are living your life as you are right now when, suddenly, one morning you wake up in a room having had your brain wiped clean of every memory before you opened your eyes. You can't remember how you got to this, what this room is, who you are, that the world exists outside this room, and so forth. With you in the room is a person that you don't recognize. The person then says to you something along these lines: "Welcome! I'm so glad you're awake. I have an offer to make you that will change everything in your life. You see, I live the perfect life – everything I do is supremely excellent and the absolute best way to live one's life. And I'm going to give you the chance to live that way, too. You are here in this room with me right now and I would love for you to stay, but first I must see if you have what it takes to live the kind of life I live. I brought you here. You're here in this room because I selected you. Because you have no memory before me, I am everything you have right now. But I promise if you do as I say, everything is going to work out."

Again, you have no clue that there is anything outside this room and for all you know, you and this person are the only two people who exist. I have a hard time believing that any of us in this situation would not want to hear the offer that this person has in mind. Let's assume that you, even if out of curiosity, ask for more information. This person then says: "Here's the bargain that I have for you. On the one hand, you can go through my character test. Beyond those doors [*he gestures to a set of double doors behind him*] is a simulation. This simulation is going to put you in a seemingly endless stream of scenarios. Those scenarios will test how you react according to my own code: if you react like I would in the scenario, you did good, and if you react any other way, you did bad. In fact, acting like me for the wrong reasons is also bad. I want to see if you have the ability to be like me in deed and spirit. Don't worry, along the way I'll send you messages to try to guide you. If you listen to those messages, you'll know what to do. When the simulation is over, I'll reward you according to how well you've done. I can't tell you totally what the reward is, but suffice to say that you get to have everything I have and can freely live the life I live."

You might then ask about what happens if you screw up and make a mistake in the simulation. Your captor says, "Never fear. There have been others who are being simulated, too. One of them is virtually a carbon copy of me, and he is going to nail/is nailing the simulation – quite literally. What I've done, though, is I've decided to punish him as if he were *the worst* simulant. He's agreed to all this, and in exchange for his willingness to be punished, we'll treat his punishment as your punishment. If you screw up, someone has already paid the ultimate price. But in exchange, you must follow his lead in the simulation. If you do what he suggests – through the messages you'll get in the simulation – your mistakes will be forgotten when the simulation is over. But if you reject him or fail to follow him, you'll have to pay the price he did. Got it?"

At this point, you might wonder if there's another option; suppose you don't want to go through this. He says, "Ah yes, that's Option 2. If you choose not to take Option 1, I'm sorry to say that you'll be destroyed. Maybe not right this second, but I'll put you in a prison until I'm done simulating others and then, when it's over, you'll be destroyed with all the others that rejected the first option. So, you can see the stakes are high here." Is there another option, you might ask – like maybe not doing this at all? "Nope. Those are your only options. You see, you're mine, I brought you here. If you reject me, you've rejected everything. So, make your decision."

Perhaps there are some rational, reasonable beings among us who would take Option 2 on principle. Maybe such people exist who can stare into the face of these options and choose destruction. But recall that even those people have no memory of a prior life – there was nothing for them before this room, this captor, and this bargain. It's hard to convince me that any thinking person would shrug and choose Option 2 under those conditions; such a person would be giving up their one shot of getting out of this room in exchange for oblivion. Instead, under the conditions as described, I think the vast majority of us would choose Option 1 because of the strong need for self-preservation.

So, let's imagine that you choose Option 1. Your captor then escorts you to the double doors and says, "Now one more thing. When you go through these doors, your brain will be wiped clean. You'll forget this room, you'll forget me, and you'll forget the purpose behind the simulation. In fact, you won't even know why you're there or where 'there' even is. But don't worry; the messages will be there, so watch for them. Good luck!" Sure enough, as you walk through the double doors, your mind is again reset. Everything beforehand is gone. Once more, you are floundering in a sea of confusion.

Now let's imagine that a few things happen in this simulation. First, depending on how eager you were to take the test, your initial starting conditions could be very good or very bad. Maybe you were really excited to take the test, so your captor set up the simulation to have people around you who already know about the test and how to beat it. You are also given good resources to pass that test; your simulated mind and body are well functioning, you aren't immediately suffering in the simulation, and the messages your captor promised are already trickling in. Then again, if you were eager, it's just as possible that the captor decided you could handle a harder test – a simulation that's full of disadvantages or a lack of access to the messages or a lot of distracting suffering. It's hard to pin down why the captor chooses the simulation he chooses, but simulated you are.

Second, everything in the simulation seems to be designed to make you *fail* the test. The simulation gives no conclusive proof that it is a simulation or that your captor exists. The messages are cryptic and inconclusive or require an awful lot of time to discover. The simulation sends you messengers that give conflicting answers, and it's difficult to sort through them. Occasionally, you hear a voice in your head that tells you to choose X in a scenario, but it's not clear whether that's a real voice or your mind playing tricks. If you are lucky, you started your simulation with individuals who can help you make sense of all this, but if you didn't, you must wait around until someone shows up to help. In the meantime, the stated goal of the test – to see whether you would react like your captor would in certain scenarios – seems to be at odds with how the simulation is functioning. Everything about the simulation makes the captor's decision look less enjoyable or meaningless, while lots of decisions your captor would call "bad" actually look pretty good in the simulation. So even if you do know the "right" answer in a scenario, you have loads of reasons *not* to choose it.

Finally, eventually someone *does* show up to tell you the message about the simulation. Maybe it's early in the simulation or very late. Maybe the message is obvious or maybe it's buried under a lot of disinformation. But eventually the message does come, and you're told the entire truth: this is a simulation, you were in another room before this simulation, there is a captor that wants you to pass this test, and you will be rewarded if you can pass it. You've screwed up thus far, but someone else has already suffered in the simulation to atone for your failures. He's created a plan for you to follow as a condition of his sacrifice. Here's a list of all the things you need to do and how to pass the test. Once again, you have no frame of reference for this. Nothing in the simulation has indicated that this particular message is accurate. In fact, you may have been flooded with lots of *other* messages that are contradictory to this one; you may have even embraced one as *the true* message, only to find out now that it was a lie.

Now, ask yourself how well you'd do under these conditions. The simulation has a range of probability, and only the captor knows what iteration you are going to face. Would you pass a test like this? Would you, without any prior knowledge, be able to discern the right path, to know which message was true, and to know whether the hints you're being given are made up? Could anyone plausibly pass this test?

Let's assume the simulation wraps up. When it's over, you are immediately brought back to the same room where you started. Your second mental reset is restored and now you can remember both the simulation itself *and* the meeting in the room with your captor before the simulation began. You remember the bargain and you remember that you took it. You also remember how well you did in the test. You remember whether you accepted the right message and acted the way you were supposed to in each given scenario. You can't now protest and claim that the scenario was unfair; after all, you agreed to it. Instead, it's time to take your reward or punishment as the captor sees fit.

The captor will then give you one of three rewards. First, a very rare, few simulants will be punished for betraying the captor. These simulants knew the answers, they were passing the test, they accepted the message, and they had everything about the simulation revealed to them because they were so committed. But they decided to rebel. If you were in that group, your captor punishes you with the same destiny you would have had if you had chosen Option 2 way back at the beginning. It's as if you didn't even take the test in the first place. So, away you go to destruction.

Second, most simulants will be given some kind of reward. These simulants struggled with the test. Maybe they didn't make it at all and never bothered to accept the message. Or maybe they accepted for a while but gave up. Or maybe they knew what they were supposed to do, but the simulation got the best of them, and they made lots of bad decisions. If you were in that group, depending on the degree of your behavior, you are sent to one of a couple of different places, all of them reasonably pleasant, where you are given everything you need to live and to do so peacefully. However, the stipulation from here on out is that you are a servant of your captor. Sure, you get a nice, cushy life, but you are never your own. You get the distinct honor of serving the captor as he conducts more simulations. You are never free to leave.

Third and finally, another exceedingly rare few simulants will have passed the test. Like the first group, they knew what they needed to do and acted accordingly. But unlike the first group, they never gave up; they doubled down and followed the message throughout the entire simulation. The simulation didn't distract them at all. They refused to give in. And even when they screwed up, they knew it was a screw up and changed course. For them, the message was always clear and living like the captor would in their situation became second nature to them. If you were in that group and did every single thing that the sacrificial simulant asked you to do, your mistakes were purged, and your captor is ready to reward you. And your reward? Well, your captor says, "Well done, good and faithful simulant. Now you get to live the life I live. Which is to say that now I will send you out...*and now you get to do your own simulations just like me.* Congratulations."

This, in a nutshell, is the plan of salvation that Mormonism shares with the world. In Mormon doctrine, we woke up at one point in the eons and suddenly had life; in the simulation, you lost your prior memory before going to the anteroom, but in Mormonism your pre-mortal self never even had a life before that. You were a blank slate on which Heavenly Father could write. And Heavenly Father gave you a similar bargain. If you failed to pass the test for any reason, you might get destruction, but more likely you'll get a cushy life as an eternal servant. If you managed to survive the outrageous conditions of the simulation and proved your worth, your reward isn't freedom, or at least not in the sense in which we think of it. Instead, your reward is to simply do what Heavenly Father has been doing – to repeat the cycle.

This realization troubled me deeply when I had it. This one cut through the cognitive dissonance of historical problems and church policies. It raised so many fundamental questions that Mormonism claimed to answer but only made worse. Why did Heavenly Father make me in the first place, if he knew I was going to go through the simulation in whatever way I was going to? Why did he need a sacrificial simulant in the form of his perfect carbon-copy, Jesus? Why would he set up the simulation in the worst possible way – why not just put everyone on the same starting conditions with less adversity and more hints? Why did he construct the simulation to make everything point to the fact that Mormonism *isn't* true? Why would he hide himself like that? Why are my chances in life so very, very low under the terms of the test? And even if I do pass it, why on earth would I want to perpetuate it?

These questions also became more practical the more I looked at every facet of Mormon doctrine. For starters, why on earth do we get the Lucifer/Satan/devil that we get out of Mormonism? A being that was there, in the moment, hearing the same bargain as the rest of us, openly rebelled and demanded to be Heavenly Father's sacrificial simulant in the defiance of Jesus? Seriously? Apparently, he took with him a third of Heavenly Father's children. There have been 117 billion humans who have been born on earth thus far; that means *at least* 58 billion and counting abandoned the test and chose Option 2; for every two humans born on earth, there was one who stayed behind. And now their fate is to wander the world, with Lucifer, working diligently to try to get people to fail the test? Why? Isn't that playing directly into Heavenly Father's hand, doesn't that actually *help* the simulation? If Lucifer and his devils simply stopped doing anything and let the simulation play out, they'd be a much bigger threat to the plan. Instead, Mormonism gives us a mustache-twirling, black-cape-wearing villain, who keeps trying to thwart the hero in the most inept and illogical way possible with idiotic minions. So much for a devil.

Moreover, at what point am I really free in all of this? Mormonism tells the world that Heavenly Father respects our freedom as agents, to choose what we wish in this life and be rewarded for it in the next. That would certainly be true if all of the options were readily clear. If my goal is to buy a car, and I truly have the freedom to choose what car to buy, I would need to know what resources I have to spend, what kinds of cars are available, how much of my resources I'll have to use to buy one, and whether the pros and cons of each car meet my interests. But using the simulation analogy, are you left with much choice in Mormonism? In a pre-mortal life, you are thrust into existence, with nothing to go on, told to make a choice between a test and destruction, and pushed through a mind-wiping Veil. Then in mortality, you are run through a lifetime simulation filled with every reason *not* to be a Mormon, given a chance either in mortality or in a brief post-mortal Spirit Prison to choose Mormonism, and then brought to Heavenly Father on Judgment Day to be assessed. Finally, he sorts you into one of three destinations, none of which are ever free from him: you're either destroyed by him, indentured to him, or told to behave like him. So much for choice.

Lastly, why do this to begin with? That was the part that became the hardest for me to process and remains the premiere question that I believe any would-be Mormon should ask. I'm supposed to believe that a loving, benevolent being, who has my best interests in mind would choose *this method* out of all other possibilities. I'm told that his goal is to "bring to pass the immortality and eternal life of man."[34] But he chose *this* way to do it? It's not even really a theological problem involving the need for a

---

[34] The Pearl of Great Price, Moses 1:39.

theodicy but a much more basic issue. Why is he doing all this? In the simulation analogy, any outside observer would scratch their head and wonder why the simulator even bothered to do all of this in the first place. Similarly, someone who follows through on the logic of Mormonism is left with all sorts of questions about Heavenly Father's motivations. Is he megalomaniacal? Unhinged? The diametric opposite of reason? Does this entertain him? Is he himself obligated to go through this process for all eternity, bound by his own cosmic simulator? So much for purpose.

***

During that two-year period of soul searching leading up to 2016, I shared these views with others, especially with other Mormons. Early on, I tried to and was often met with one of two very unsatisfying answers to these questions (or any other question that one may have about Mormonism). First, I was often told that these questions were not necessary for salvation and god had revealed only the most essential information to his prophets; everything else was just superfluous. This answer always seemed disingenuous to me. For starters, it was a version of the "true Scotsman" fallacy. Which were the "true questions" that could be counted as necessary to my salvation? I was constantly encouraged to go to the temple and study the symbolism there, to read the scriptures for esoteric messages from Heavenly Father, to fast and pray for revelation that would pattern my life, and to seek out the higher truths of the gospel. One of the core beliefs of Mormonism is that the worthier one is, the more truth Heavenly Father will reveal. Every prophet in every era had explained that he "will yet reveal many great and important things"[35] to his children. And yet some questions were off limits? These questions were OK to ask because they were salvation-oriented, but these ones weren't? That response seemed like a really easy way to keep moving the goalposts in any discussion about the plan of salvation.

That answer was also problematic for another reason. I had been told and had taught that Mormonism can answer the three most fundamental questions of life: where were we before, why are we here, where are we going.[36] In fact, I also taught others that Joseph Smith had entered a grove of trees in Palmyra, New York, with those very questions in his mind and had begun the lengthy process of getting answers after Heavenly Father appeared to him. The current message of Mormonism was the culmination of that process. And yet, the more one sits with the logic of the plan of salvation, the less it addresses those questions. Sure, before life, we were conceived as spirit children by Heavenly Father, but were we anywhere before that or did we spring into existence one day? Why did he create us in the first place? Sure, I was here on earth to be tested, but why this particular form of testing – why, of all the methods, this one? And sure, in the next life, I'll go to some final destination which will most likely be pleasant in many ways, but to what end? Why is it that the best I can hope for is to live an eternal life where I duplicate what Heavenly Father had done for me? The most I can expect is an eternity of creating more spirit

---

[35] *The Articles of Faith*, No. 9.
[36] Uchtdorf, Dieter F. "O How Great the Plan of Our God!," *Semiannual Conference* (October 2016).

children only to watch most of them end up either rebelling or being my servants. Those answers to life's big questions are no more satisfying to me than the answers a Catholic, a Jew, or a Hindu might offer. And honestly, all these are kind of silly.

The second response I often heard when I brought all of this up is that there are no answers to those questions, but that Mormonism is nevertheless true. This was a response I was instructed to give as a missionary when faced with difficult questions; rather than engage the question head on, I was trained to tell people, "I don't know the answer to that, but I do know the Mormon church is true. I can testify of that because..." with the gap being filled by something like *The Book of Mormon*'s authenticity or Joseph Smith's divine calling. A similar version of this is "Well, your ancestors believed it..." or "So-and-so Famous Mormon believes it, and they're no dummy." This response – what Mormons often call "having a testimony" or "testifying" – is a bare assertion that Mormonism is true. This logical fallacy – the *ad populum* fallacy – makes truth entirely dependent on the number or quality of people who believe it; the irony of such thinking is that a large number *disbelieving* an idea is rarely seen as counterevidence of truth. Yet, Mormons place significant value on this assertion-based reasoning. For example, children are taught to "gain a testimony" before they get baptized or, at least, before they serve missions or get married. Once a month, during the first Sunday sacrament service, Mormons are encouraged to participate in an "open mic" meeting wherein anyone can get up and share their testimony to publicly reaffirm their commitment to the Mormon church. And a prerequisite for entry in a Mormon temple is an interview with a bishop and stake president in which a person is asked detailed questions that essentially assess that person's testimony.

The reality is that this fail-safe answer was always the answer – indeed, the *only* answer – that could ever be given from a Mormon in the face of any serious problem within Mormon doctrine. The simple reality is that there *are* core, fundamental questions about Mormonism that have yet to be publicly and definitively answered. All that one has left in the face of those questions is a testimony. Although I had spent many years offering that same answer when questioned by others, I slowly found that it wasn't offering me much in the way of resolution for a couple of reasons. For one, that answer was often cover for failing to acknowledge the problem I had raised. These doctrinal inconsistencies and holes were very real problems at the center of Mormonism. And yet the "But I believe it" answer was totally incongruent with the question. You believe what – that there's a hole in Mormonism? You believe that everything else masks over that hole? I fail to see a satisfying connection between a person's sincere belief in a thing and the critical inspection of that belief. But on another level, such an answer didn't offer much in the way of proving anything. I was never sure what I was supposed to do with another person's assertion that they believed. When you tell me that you believe a thing, you haven't demonstrated to me that that thing is true or real. You've just proved to me that *you believe* it's true or real, a fact that I will never contest; far be it for me to tell you that you don't believe. But like witness testimony in a trial, all I can really do with that assertion is acknowledge that you see the world a certain way and assess that against the contradictory assertions of others plus whatever direct or circumstantial evidence is available. In short, I can't really do much with your testimony.

It was against this backdrop that I finally started seeking professional help. For years, I had put off the worsening symptoms of my OCD, the mental cycle of failure, the years of mental checking on my worthiness and cleanliness, and the general dissatisfaction I constantly felt about myself. The brief but powerful suicidal moment at the train station in Maryland was a wakeup call and, at Emily's urging, I finally sought help. At first, it was difficult to name the problem; unpacking 30+ years of development and inner debates didn't happen overnight. It also required a significant amount of education for my therapist, who had very little knowledge of Mormon beliefs and culture. But over time, I got better at explaining what I felt, why I felt it, and how it fit within my history. I went to therapy because I was out of ideas; everything else I had tried – prayer and faith, research from spiritual and academic sources, conversations with others, and so forth – just hadn't worked. I thought that therapy would be the thing that finally put my mind at ease and let me settle back into the life I had wanted. This would all be a blip on the radar in a few years.

But as I said at the beginning of this chapter, things hit critical mass in the summer of 2016. As I sat on the couch facing my therapist, about a quarter of the way through one of our sessions, she paused to look at her notes. I could hear the clock ticking in the background, and I could feel that slight flush in my cheeks that I always had when I started sharing with her what was on my mind that week. She asked me to take a step back and assess the last several months of therapy; she wanted me to look back on why I had come in the first place and decide whether or not it was helping. She recounted to me from her notes some of the issues I had raised: my high aspirations for my spirituality, my sense of failure at meeting any of them, my doctrinal questions, my OCD and depression, and my general dissatisfaction with the last several years of my life. She asked whether I saw any common denominator in all of this. She leaned back in her chair, locked her eyes on me, and said quietly: "I want you to pause for just a moment and entertain this question: Is being a Mormon making you happy?"

I broke down.

2. Apatheistic About What?

This is perhaps the lengthiest part of my story, and I apologize if it has felt tedious. But I have belabored it for a crucial reason. I have used my own story to illustrate the distinction between apatheism and zealotry – from the perspective of intensity and from the perspective of reciprocity and exceptionalism. My story shows the length to which the zealot attitude can go. I have offered the details in this phase of my life to illustrate the shift in my attitude with regard to my beliefs – a painful, frustrating, and existential shift. In the following chapter, I will show how this tumultuous phase has transitioned over time to a place of peace and self-love.

But I share this part of my story for another reason. I have shown what apatheism is as a competitor to zealotry, but now I want to show how apatheism can be directed to a range of possible beliefs. In my own story, one of the major problems that led to my breakdown was that my zealot attitude toward my beliefs. Yet, not all of my beliefs at a given time carried that zealot attitude; my zealotry about Heavenly Father's interaction with me, for instance, was low, while my zealotry about his general plan of salvation was extremely high. Sometimes there could be a major shift in my attitude between those beliefs. It is a feature of religious attitudes that they are not static and not always of the same degree, depending on the belief to which they are tied. My two-year emotional collapse illustrates how my zealot attitude toward some beliefs eclipsed the less extreme attitudes to the detriment of my well-being.

For this reason, I want to abstract from my own experience and highlight at least three beliefs to which apatheism may be directed. Just as one can be an apatheist and still be a religious observer, one can be an apatheist about some things but not about others when it comes to religious beliefs. Categorizing religious beliefs around common threads is always challenging, so the categories I am proposing here are not written in stone. However, I believe they serve as a helpful conceptual tool for orienting ourselves to religious beliefs; by addressing these categories, one could ask, "How do I feel toward this belief?" As I described in the first chapters, these "Big Three" religious beliefs are: (1) the existence of a deity, (2) that deity's interaction with the known universe, and (3) one's loyalty to that deity. Without getting into theological debates, I want to describe what I mean by each of these beliefs.

a. Belief 1: The existence of a deity

Of the three potential religious beliefs, the existence of a deity is perhaps the most straightforward and obvious. It is the most basic of questions for a religion to answer whether there is a godly figure or figures that should be worshipped or, at least, acknowledged. But beyond mere existence, this belief can encompass a few related concepts.

For example, it could include the *origin* of a deity. Is this deity eternal or temporary? Did the deity spring from nothing? Is this deity here, in the sense that it can be understood empirically, or is this deity a concept? It could also include the *type* of deity. Is this deity singular, a trinity, a pantheon, or something else? Is this deity human-like, animalistic, or an amorphous entity? Does the deity possess what we would consider to be an identity: a gender, race, sexuality, and so forth? Is this deity fallible, the most powerful, or all powerful? Is it an idiot god or a supremely intelligent being? Is it self-interested, supremely altruistic, or completely devoid of what we would call emotions? Finally, this belief could also include *evidence* of the deity in question. Has it left any signs of its existence? What parts of the universe point to this deity being there? Has it purposefully hidden itself from human understanding? Is it so far beyond the boundaries of thought that evidence is a meaningless concept when applied to it?

Whatever flavor they may take, the existence questions are those which are often most easily discernable as religious. In many cases, these questions are the first place where one faces the problem of how much energy to direct toward them. They serve as a starting point for everything else that follows. How one positions themselves attitudinally toward the existence questions can set the tone for their religious intensity and any exceptionalism claims they may have. But religious belief isn't *solely* about a god's existence.

b. Belief 2: A deity's interaction with the known universe

Religious beliefs to which apatheism can be directed can also include those that explain how an existent deity interacts with the universe. These are separate beliefs from existence. The fact that a deity exists does not necessarily imply that it has any interaction with the world whatsoever. Many faiths do believe in such an interactive being, to greater or lesser degrees, but the two beliefs are not identical. By way of an extreme example: One could be a Lovecraftian cultist and believe that the universe is a dream sequence of the blind-idiot god, Azathoth, who is completely incapable of interacting with his dream.

Like the existence question, the interaction question contains multiple sub-questions. For example, interaction could include a *creation* narrative. Did the deity create the universe? If so, did it do so consciously or accidentally? Did it create the universe separately from itself or is the universe a part of the deity? How did the deity create the universe? Did it have help? What did it make the universe from if anything? Can it unmake the universe and, if so, what prevents it from doing so? Does the deity still hold the universe in order or did it "start up the machine" and walk away from it? Is the universe it created a literal one or is all that we see a series of experiences being fed into our minds à la the simulation example I provided earlier? Does the deity have a purpose in mind for the universe or is the deity indifferent to its creation? If there is a purpose, what is it?

Additionally, the interaction question can include *human placement* in the deity's universe. Were humans a product of creation or an accidental tag along? Are we special to the deity or are all things, living or inert, equally valuable to the deity? If we are also created, how did the deity do so? To what end, if any? Does the deity have a goal in mind for us or is the deity indifferent to our fate? Did our humanity spring into existence at birth and will it snuff out at death? Or is a human being existent before birth and/or after death? Are there layers to existence that the deity has hidden from humans or is the known universe everything that we can observe?

Finally, the interaction question can be *human involvement* in the deity's universe. Does the deity communicate with humans? If so, how? Is this form of communication a two-way line; can activities like prayer, fasting, meditation, and so forth link us with this deity? If I ask the deity for help, will it intervene on my behalf? Can I change its mind or is it the same mind from beginning to end? Are the events that happen in my life ones that the deity purposefully designs to happen? Or are these pleasant and unpleasant situations I find myself in a product of the natural order of the universe? Does this deity have a personal plan for me, does it know me intimately, and does it wish to tailor its guidance to my choices and goals? Or does the deity have a general plan for humanity, and I must find my own place within that?

Like the existence beliefs, interaction beliefs are extensive and can take many forms. But unlike the existence question, the variability of answers to these questions is significantly more diverse. For example, even those religions that can all be called Christian – all of which accept the belief in an existing god who created the known universe and has a plan for humanity – have a wide variety of answers to the interaction question. Calvinist sects have long taught that a person's purpose is to discover what the god has planned for them – a plan that is fixed and unchanging. Meanwhile, Catholic sects accept the notion that this god can be angry or pleased with behavior and, therefore, is able to be propitiated. Evangelical and non-denominational sects teach that simply accepting Jesus is enough to satisfy the god's justice. Alignment around a particular existence belief doesn't mean that one has to also align around interaction beliefs.

c. Belief 3: One's loyalty to a deity

If existence beliefs are fundamental to religion and interaction beliefs are the ways in which religion diversifies, then loyalty beliefs are the more practical, day-to-day beliefs of a faith. At one level, these beliefs are organizational; if I'm a Mormon, I believe I should behave in X way, which will be different than what a Muslim or Jain will believe. Group identity plays a substantial role on this front. But at another level, these beliefs are also personal; even among Mormons, the commitment that Mormonism requires to Heavenly Father is going to be different depending on the person. How one interprets and applies doctrine will have a profound impact on how one views their loyalty to a deity.

Like the prior two beliefs, loyalty beliefs can raise a multitude of questions. Some of these questions are *behavioral*. How does my deity want me to think? What am I allowed to say without offending this deity? Does the deity have a source of knowledge I can look to for guidance on how I should act? Are my duties to other people different depending on how my deity views those people? If I don't always follow my deity's guidance, is there any way to rectify the mistake? If others make similar mistakes, what is my obligation to them, especially if they don't share my beliefs? Will my deity's expectations of me remain fixed throughout my life or does my deity mold its behavioral code to fit my circumstances? All of these questions involve the way in which my loyalty is expressed by my thoughts and actions.

Other questions are much more *metaphysical*. What is my status with regard to my deity? Does it love me? Hate me? Is it indifferent to me? Can I make my deity sad or angry or pleased? If so, how can I do or not do so? Can this deity perform miracles in my life if I act a certain way? Will it grant me certain supernatural powers if I please it? Regardless of the plan my deity has for the rest of the world, where do I personally fit in it? Can I meet this deity in mortality? Will I do so after I am dead? How many of my decisions do I need to adjust to accomplish whatever goals my deity has in mind for me?

While existence beliefs are classic problems for religious knowledge (the X-axis I described in Chapter 1), loyalty beliefs, on the surface, look more attitudinal. One might say that having an attitude toward knowledge claims about deity's existence is one thing, but beliefs about loyalty are quite another; don't those in themselves define how much zealotry or apatheism I should adopt? In other words, if I accept that I should be loyal to something, wouldn't that always define the level of my attitude toward it? I would argue that it does not for a very simple reason: loyalty beliefs do not always translate into behavior. For instance, the vast majority of Americans believe that patriotism is a valuable civic virtue. On the question of loyalty to America, many share the same level knowledge: we know that loyalty is a good thing and that political participation is important. And yet, despite this overwhelmingly shared knowledge claim, the range of attitudes with regard to this knowledge claim is very broad. Some individuals portray an attitude of intensity with regard to patriotism – a willingness to fight and die for the country no matter what. On the opposite extreme, some individuals see no need to vote or participate in civil discourse while still being loyal Americas who love their country. Pick your favorite relationships that involve some claims about loyalty – family and marriage, hobbies and entertainment, professions – and you'll likely find that knowing one's duty of loyalty does not always translate into one kind of attitude. Just knowing that one needs to be loyal to something does not produce similar results among people; attitude plays a mediating role.

3. Making the Apatheist Connection

Apatheism can be applied to all of these three beliefs on the basis of intensity and reciprocity or exceptionalism. In terms of intensity, I could feel an attitude of deep fervor toward all three beliefs. I may passionately believe in a god, believe that it possesses certain qualities, that interacts regularly with the world, and that I should be as loyal as possible to it to avoid its wrath. I could, in essence, be a comprehensive zealot on all religious beliefs. The picture of such a zealot is good fodder for any novel involving cults or any murder documentary involving some religious fanatic. But intensity does not have to be directed to all of these beliefs, either. I can imagine a scenario in which a person could deeply and passionately attach to beliefs about god existence; such a person would be unwavering in their belief and share it with anyone who is willing to listen. But such a person may not feel as equally intense about his or her loyalty. They may know that such a being expects loyalty, but in their private life they may be lax on the moral code. Or they may happily express their belief in god at a supremely intense level, but when it comes to changing the world or expecting others to share their beliefs, they may be indifferent. Granted, certain combinations of beliefs may be more likely to produce such intensity; it may be more likely that believing in an existent, interactive deity that demands loyalty produces intensity. But it's far too strong a statement to say that one must always have the same level of intensity about every religious belief.

Moreover, these beliefs are ripe for the other feature of apatheism, the commitment to reciprocity versus the demand for exceptionalism. I might very well claim to know that a god exists, that it interacts with the universe and, particularly, humans, and that this god demands loyalty. I can imagine a person who is deeply convinced of the truthfulness of all of those knowledge claims. I can even imagine that one patterns all of his or her life around such claims. Yet, such a person does not necessarily automatically claim to be exceptional. Such a person might believe that these claims are operative in his or her private life, but that in public life, these claims are secondary to the need to get along with others, preserve order, and accomplish whatever justice can be achieved in a world of a diversity of opinions. For example, a person might believe that an existent, interactive deity expects them to conduct animal sacrifice. Yet, that person might live in a part of the world in which animal cruelty laws do not permit such activities. That person might demand a special exemption from such laws, believing that they are exceptional among the rest of us. Or they might just as easily shrug and move on, knowing that any demand they make for exception could just as easily be countered with a multitude of others who claim such exceptions.

Moreover, belief is not all or nothing when it comes to reciprocity. I could claim that my deity is particularly interactive, that I'm certain my deity is orchestrating events in the world, and that this deity will explode with wrath unless I am given the opportunity to share my beliefs. And yet, when it comes to loyalty beliefs, it's possible that such a person would be supportive of other religious people being given the right to worship their deity in their own way. Such a person would care deeply about recognition of their beliefs about god's existence but be indifferent about how that cashes out in terms of human behavior. If one part of the test for apatheism is the degree to which one allows for reciprocity and does or does not claim exceptionalism, then its logically possible for that to take many forms based on the underlying claim of religious knowledge.

These features of apatheism can also be much more personal and intimately wrapped up in a person's internal life. As I discussed in the public/private distinction, zealotry and apatheism can display themselves in how one feels toward oneself and to one's faith generally. A person can have an apatheistic attitude toward the priority of these beliefs in his or her decision making, in the relationships that they might form, and in the way they view themselves. Such a person would likely not let such beliefs determine all of their goals or define what relationships they might have. Such a person might also give themselves some space to grow into their beliefs and to adapt to changing circumstances. An attitude of zealotry would place these beliefs at their highest possible priority; unless a plan of action or a relationship or my own mental state is not consistent with any or all of these religious beliefs, it should be avoided or minimized. Attitudes on this front can be expressed both externally and internally.

This discussion leads me back to the portion of my story that I shared earlier in this chapter. As my story shows, I had adopted the attitude of a zealot throughout much of my growing up years. When it came to the "Big Three" beliefs, I ran the full spectrum. In terms of existence, Heavenly Father was real, he created the universe spiritually and physically, and he possessed a particular love for humanity. He was our father and all of us his children. In terms of interaction, Heavenly Father was pervasive in the universe. At times, the extent of that pervasiveness to me seemed very large: world events, individual choices, problems and successes, and so forth all seemed to emanate from him. At other times, I believed he was a benevolent guide, who painstakingly kept out of most human affairs unless needed. In terms of loyalty, I believed I owed him everything – complete and total submission. The highest honor I believed that I could be given was to know that I had so proved to Heavenly Father that he could trust me that he would grant me a life that he had. And I believed that this meant intervening in the lives of others. On all fronts, my attitude was such that I felt these beliefs made me exceptional. Others could follow whatever rules they wished; man's laws were one thing. But I was under a much different authority.

At the same time, this attitude had a destructive effect on my internal life. I had so prioritized these beliefs that I had neglected to take seriously my own mental health. I was so committed to reconciling my beliefs with themselves that I nearly threw away my life under an Acela train careening through Maryland. Moreover, my attitude was such that any mistake – any failure – was at the very least lost time in my eternal progression and maybe even years beyond repair. Even when my beliefs began to shift as I encountered a diverse world beyond Idaho and Utah and faced a fresh set of problems within Mormonism, my old zealotry refused to diminish. My beliefs changed, but my attitude had not. The old zealot was clinging on for dear life.

As I hope my story has shown thus far, belief in any or all of the "Big Three" does not mandate a particular attitude. It so happened that my own zealotry aligned with my beliefs at some moments, but at others, it did not. My example should serve as an entry point to explore how these attitudes and beliefs interact in the lives of other religious or non-religious people. Assessing one's beliefs or the beliefs of others is one thing, but unpacking their attitude toward those beliefs requires an additional layer of analysis. In the following chapter, I will offer a tentative conclusion on my own story and illustrate why all of this discussion of apatheism and zealotry matters.

Who Cares?

Men never do evil so completely and cheerfully as when they do it from religious conviction.
– Blaise Pascal

1. My Beloved Son, in Whom I Am Well Pleased

Lewis Black has this great bit about the difference between the Old and New Testament versions of god. After pointing out the obvious differences between the violent, vindictive Old Testament god and the love-oriented New Testament version, Black says this: "I don't know what happened to God over time, how He matured. Maybe He went to an anger management class. Or maybe just the birth of His son calmed Him down." I don't know about god, but that sure worked for me.

Starting with that moment in therapy in 2016, my relationship to Mormonism changed forever. In answer to the question, "Was Mormonism making me happy?" I was stumped. Before, I would not have hesitated: "Of course, it's making me happy! It's the plan of happiness, after all; if I happen to be overwhelmed with the expectations Mormonism has placed on me, that's incidental." But now, 10 years out of missionary service and in a loving relationship, I wasn't so sure. Was this happiness that I felt every day? Were the sleepless nights and the constant self-regulation in my brain what people meant when they said they were happy? Was sitting in church or reading the scriptures bringing me any kind of peace? If so, it did not seem obvious anymore.

That question prompted months of soul searching – a period of time that did not get any easier. The analogy I would offer is that for much of my life, this superstructure had been built around me. Like a person in a well-designed, well-decorated building, being a Mormon had been safe and comfortable. There were four walls around me and roof over my head to protect me from the lies and deceits of a world run by Satan. In this philosophical home, I could be confident that I would have peace. But the last several years culminating in this basic question had destroyed that superstructure. It had started with small cracks and chips of paint. I had little questions that could not be answered satisfactorily. Or there were Mormon church policies that did not feel right to me – the lesser status of women in the church, the treatment of LGBTQ folks, the disproportion between the church's wealth and charity. And then it was the bigger questions that made me realize that this superstructure was an illusion – the inconsistencies in Mormon doctrine, the inadequacy of answers that Mormon dogma claimed were so crucial, and so forth. When it was all said and done, I was mentally standing in an empty lot, exposed to the elements, the building having evaporated around me. Was I happy?

Feeling completely unmoored and without anything to grip to, the next several moments were ugly to say the least. Professionally, I was feeling accomplished and successful as a Ph.D.

student, but personally, behind closed doors, I was floundering. For starters, if Mormonism wasn't true, why was I avoiding things like coffee, tea, and alcohol? Why was I so worried about the media I consumed? Why was I working so hard to watch every word, thought, and deed? Like a person on an intense diet who has suddenly been let loose in a massive buffet, I saw no reason to pass up any opportunity to experience life as I thought others had experienced. After all, I had missed out, hadn't I? Everyone else in the world – the "normal" people – lived this way. Hadn't they had their teen years, full of dumb mistakes and individuation? It was my turn; I deserved it, didn't I?

Worst of all, I began to significantly question my relationships, one in particular. Many of my relationships had been a product of Mormonism. I had coworkers and friends outside of the Mormon church, but some of my best and most long-lived relationships were with people I had met because of Mormonism. My marriage most of all had been a product of Mormonism. Emily and I knew each other because we had been in the same Mormon circles, we dated under Mormon conditions, we got married young because we believed Mormon doctrine, and we were married in a Mormon temple. But if Mormonism wasn't true, then why was I friends with all of these people? Why was I married to Emily?

Emily had her own questions and was going through her own faith journey at the same time, but hers was slow and methodical. She still clung to the culture of the church and was terrified of reprisals from friends and family for leaving. I, on the other hand, had careened down this path at breakneck speed. It was a recipe for months of conflict and a complex mess of emotions. On the one hand, I wanted to be committed to Emily. We wanted to start a family together. We wanted to grow old together. We had been the best of friends over our 10-year marriage. But on the other hand, was this our dealbreaker? How could we survive such a massive shift in our relationship? If she was going to remain Mormon for her own reasons, did that mean our marriage was through? Should we have ever even *been* together? Without Mormonism, was what we had called "love" for so long just an illusion, too?

Years after the fact, I look back on those months with a mixture of shame and understanding. A lot of that time period is a blur, buried in the back of my subconscious where I don't have to acknowledge it. I acted as though my marriage was over and as though longtime friends were now strangers to me. I said hurtful things to Emily and family members. I made health decisions that I'm still paying the price for. I ripped through my life with the attitude of someone who has "earned" this moment and the rest of the world be damned. And what's most ironic is that, outwardly, most people would not have even been aware of the wildfire raging in my private life.

At the same time, I now have a glimmer of understanding for myself, one that I have had to learn over time. I can recognize now that I was achieving a self-fulfilling prophecy. I had told others for many years that, without the Mormon church, it was only a matter of time before a person became a monster. When the scaffolding came down, I subconsciously assumed that that was what I needed to become. I had accepted the "either/or" of Mormonism. I had tried the "either," and now I was going to bathe in the "or" – and I was going to give it the same intense exceptionalism that had fueled me most of my life. I had defined myself by Mormonism for so long, that when it appeared to no longer have value in my life, I figured I needed to remake my whole person. I look back and see someone who had "happiness" defined for him for so long that when that definition slipped, all he had was to grasp at whatever came his way. I also see someone who could not let the old intensity and sense of exceptionalism die down.

A tool that is often used in therapy is the "child within" technique. The theory is that emotions that we feel define us are only symptoms of something deeper. Often, what lies at the root of depression, anxiety, anger, and self-hatred, is that part of us that is afraid and alone. I am only an audience member and not an expert when it comes to psychology, but I have learned from enough professionals that many of our adult behaviors are coping mechanisms we acquired as children when we were scared. So, the theory goes, finding that child within – looking back on that scared, innocent person – deflates the blame and guilt, and lets a person heal.

What I saw in myself during this phase was just that: a child who had hung on to Mormonism; when it was gone, he was terrified and needed the adult version of himself to help him find safety again. Slowly, painfully, and with a tremendous amount of real love from the most important people in my life, I began to see that this real, vulnerable person was not defined by the beliefs he had or the definitions that had been given to him. He was defined by the person he was, to himself and to others. I will not in any way suggest that that process is complete; I think the psychological literature demonstrates that this is a lifetime process and the very essence of being human. But I can safely say that those darks months are in the rearview mirror.

Still, I was not publicly and definitively ready to separate from Mormonism. During this period of soul searching, I often wondered if I had been right all along. My marriage nearly failed, my health had suffered, and my other relationships were in flux. Wasn't that the cautionary tale of Mormonism? Perhaps this was Heavenly Father's warning to me. Without the Spirit guiding me, was I doomed to cycle of self-destruction? The old part of my brain was still afraid to finally "call it" on Mormonism. Out of respect for Emily's own faith journey and the general need to feel some sense of stability, I hung on as long as I could. I could justify it as an outward commitment to save face with family, friends, and my community, while internally I could be my authentic self. I would be the good Mormon boy in public to hold together the person people thought I was, and I would privately remind myself that none of this made any sense. And I did that very well…for a while.

***

In early December 2018, three years after moving to California and starting graduate school, Emily's water broke. The irony of that moment was that I was right in the middle of cleaning up water that had flooded into our small apartment in Davis, CA, during a period of very heavy rain. There I was with a shop vac and mold-preventing chemicals doing my best to clean up our carpet until the landlord slouched around to fix it, when she yelled from upstairs. "My water just broke!" Water, water, everywhere.

No one who hasn't lived it can fully appreciate that combination of excitement, chaos, fear, and total ineptness that follows an announcement like that. Emily and I had developed a whole plan that we would follow on our way to the hospital, timed right down to the second; that plan got drowned in the deluge that followed. Looking back as a seasoned parent does, I chuckle at our chaos. We threw together what we had. We forgot to lock the house - twice. I dropped Emily's suitcase multiple times. At one point, I nearly knocked myself out on the door to our garage. When it was all said and done, we threw everything into our Prius and headed for the hospital.

What followed was 48 hours of labor and delivery. Again, once you've had your first child, you wonder why you were afraid in the moment, but there's just no telling that to the mind of two new parents who have never watched the irrationality of pregnancy and childbirth. I stayed by Emily through the long, two-day labor, and I like to believe I accomplished *something* while I was there. But in reality, it was Emily's strength and determination that did all the work; I was just lucky to be there. It had taken fertility treatments, years of disappointments and missed successes, and a whole lot of love to get us there. What finally brought a child into our life was a doula who held Emily's hand, a nurse that kept screaming push, and Emily's ability to kick the hell out of a problem when she needs to. I just got to be the one standing there with my hands open when our son finally appeared.

I don't know what other fathers have felt in a moment like that. I'm sure the full range of human emotions is possible in a delivery room. But I can't speak to their experiences because all I have is my own. Two things happened to me in that moment which have forever changed the course of my life. The first is that suddenly everything in my life came into sharp, clear, and well-defined focus. Throughout the last six years, I had been "looking through a glass darkly," but in that moment I *saw* for the first time in years. I saw Emily for the first time – not the Emily I married, but the Emily who was there, right at that moment, tear stained and exhausted. I saw myself standing at the foot of the hospital bed, with a couple of nurses showing me what to do as my son came into the world. I saw myself not as I had been, but as I am – a man who had taken the internal, "little boy" version of himself into his arms and told him that everything was going to be OK now. And I saw the face of my son – small and innocent, but full of courage and life. Although my eyes were full of tears, I saw more clearly than I ever had.

The second is that I heard a voice. It wasn't the cosmic, spiritual being I thought I had been hearing most of my life. It wasn't the one reminding me what I had done wrong and what all I had yet to do to earn some celestial being's approval. It wasn't the one that had made lists and spreadsheets of goals for me to accomplish. It wasn't the one that had narrated my life and given a director's cut commentary on all the events that I saw around, complete with criticism of the non-Mormon world. No, this was just me – my own thoughts finally put into words. As I looked down at my son, I reflected on the life that he was going to live – a vision of all the possibilities he would face flooded my brain in milliseconds. I saw raw, untouched humanity lying there in my hands, pale, weak, and covered in blood. I saw a little boy who deserved his own life, who hadn't chosen the conditions of his birth and deserved a full range of options. The responsibility I felt toward him was not a crushing burden, but a mantle of trust and peace. And clear as day, the voice in my head said:

"You are not a Mormon anymore."

2. The Natural Man is an Enemy to God

Throughout this book, I have talked about zealotry in isolation as if it were something that a person could just pick up like a hobby or a profession. It is probably true that a person living alone, completely separated from others, could develop a zealot lifestyle on their own, without the help of a priest or sitting on a pew. But in the journey toward zealotry, priests and pews certainly seem to help. That point brings me to the final piece of apatheism: why it matters.

An attitude toward religious beliefs, whether apatheistic or zealot, is not developed overnight. It is formed after educating oneself about the beliefs and testing them through action. In this way, zealotry has the upper hand over apatheism: places where religious beliefs are taught and modeled are often good incubators for zealots, while there are not exactly dedicated places for apatheistic values. There are probably many reasons for why this is: group think, the need for a community, self-selection by zealots into more extreme faiths, and doctrine itself. I would like to add one more reason to that list, namely the ability of religious organizations to redefine concepts differently from their natural, intuitive sense. I can hazard a few examples from my own experience.

Take the concept "tolerance." Intuitively, tolerance is not a difficult idea. In terms of human development and the success of our species, tolerance means, at a minimum, the notion of "live and let live." We have a good sense for when injustice is committed; if you work hard to grow some apples in your backyard, and I come through in the middle of the night and take all of them, you feel a sense of injustice. It is not fair that you should work hard to enjoy something you love, only to have it taken from you by someone who did not put in the same amount of work. True, it is often said that life isn't fair. But much of the reason why human beings form relationships, societies, and states is to avoid injustice. We have a sense that if each of us is going to be able to live the way we wish, there will need to be some set of rules – legal or ethical – that we all recognize and abide by so that we don't have to fear one another. We can rest easy that, when a conflict arises, we can appeal to these rules and have the support of one another to rectify this injustice. If a person elects not to be a part of that community, the community has every right to expel them.

Call it a "social contract" or "culture" or "customs" or whatever you wish, humanity has made it as long as it has by depending on this basic sense of fairness. Tolerance is just another expression of this sense of fairness in terms of belief. I want to have my beliefs and I recognize that you do, too, so I'll agree to stay out of your way if you stay out of mine. This natural definition of tolerance is fairly straightforward. Even if it is difficult to conform to that definition in hard cases, we still do it an awful lot.

But zealot faiths, which lack the reciprocity that apatheism has, teach their adherents that tolerance means something else. For zealot faiths, tolerance is always unidirectional: *they* deserve tolerance, but everyone else does not. For example, Mormonism claims the right to send individuals into nations, communities, and homes to teach people why everything they've known, religiously speaking, is wrong. Mormonism's entire message to the world is that *everyone* else is wrong; even if some faiths get a few things right, they're still ultimately wrong because Heavenly Father hasn't given those faiths the same priesthood he has given to the Mormon church. One has to wonder, though, how the Mormon community would react if, say, a group of Evangelical Christians sent thousands of missionaries to Mormon doorsteps throughout Utah and Idaho and called them all to repentance. I can hazard a guess that it would not be met with equanimity for very long.

At times, Mormonism has claimed a special exemption to do whatever it wishes without regard for the people in its path. For instance, when Joseph Smith identified Jackson County, Missouri as the place where Christ would return and the city of Zion would be built, hundreds of Mormons settled in the area, completely upsetting the balance of political and cultural power in the area. Out of misinformation and their own zealotry, many Missourians in the area attacked the Mormon settlers. This led to retaliation, legal infighting, violence, and unnecessary animosity between Mormons and their neighbors. At one point and under the guise of revelation, Joseph marched a group of 200 odd volunteers to Missouri from Mormon headquarters in Kirtland, Ohio, with the goal to "redeem Zion." When it became clear that they were outnumbered and the effort was fruitless due to the years of resentment, Joseph disbanded his militia. The event accomplished nothing other than to purge from the young church those who were not prepared to follow Joseph without question. No community deserves violence and the bigoted, slave-owning Southerners who attacked the Mormons deserve every condemnation. There are absolutely no apologies sufficient to justify their abhorrent behavior. At the same time, you have to scratch your head when Joseph, a Northerner alive during a time of intense regional animosity, looked at a map and said, "That seems like a good spot to set up are weird faith; I bet those brain-dead bigots will love us." How would Utah Mormons react today if, say, the Islamic Brotherhood did the same with Salt Lake City and sent 1200 Muslim jihadists to live next door?[37]

In every case, from missionary work to doctrine to political statements to the things it does with its money, the Mormon church's stance has always been one of asking for tolerance. The

---

[37] In actuality, we really don't have to wonder. The story of the founding of Rajneeshpuram in Antelope, Oregon, by a group of devotees to the Indian mystic, Bhagwan Shree Rajneesh, is a cautionary tale that this sort of thing is not very far in the rearview mirror of history. The intense animosity between the Rajneeshees — a fanatic group with unusual practices and worldviews — and the local Oregonians — steeped in a xenophobic cowboy culture similar to my hometown of Southeastern Idaho — is about as close to a contemporary comparison to what happened between the Mormons and Missourians as you can find.

rest of the world is told constantly to let the church be, as if Mormonism were no greater concern that a small Amish settlement in Pennsylvania. I heard it all the time growing up and still hear it from dedicated Mormons after some unfavorable news coverage or some documentary is released or some academic or politician turns their attention to Mormonism: "Please just tolerate us. What have we ever done to you?" When individuals who have left the Mormon church give speeches or write books about their experience, you will hear the standard phrase: "They can leave Mormonism, but they just can't leave it alone."

This attitude runs so deep that even events totally unrelated to Mormonism are seen as an attack on the faith. As I have described in other chapters, Mormonism teaches that this life is a testing ground and that in a pre-mortal life, we were presented with Heavenly Father's plan for testing us. When a third of us rebelled, they were sent to earth as Satan and his devils. Mormonism describes that rebellion as the "War in Heaven" and reminds any who will listen that this war is still going on in the private and public life of people. So, it is not too much of a logical leap for Mormonism to look at anything inconsistent with its tenets as yet another Satanic salvo in that conflict. In the 19th Century, it was laws against polygamy and underage marriage. In the early 20th Century, it was women's rights and communism. In the late 20th Century, it was civil rights and sexual permissiveness. Now, in the 21st Century, it's gay marriage, insurance laws, taxes, and multiculturalism. To the Mormon church and its leadership, *everything* is either for or against Mormonism.

This one-sided idea of tolerance, in which anything I do to you is acceptable because I'm right and anything you do to me is not because you're wrong, is at the heart of the persecution narrative that zealot faiths like Mormonism depend on. As a young man in Idaho, I believed fervently that "people out there" hated Mormons and that they wanted to take away our religion. That helped me survive all those years of rejection as a missionary; it wasn't that Mormonism was wrong, it's that they hated us. This was an excellent reinforcement tool that zealot faiths need to deal with hostility; any adversity I encountered was just further proof that Mormonism was right.

I won't belabor that topic any further than to point out how far this behavior deviates from our natural sense of tolerance. Tolerance is justice-oriented and rooted in the belief that everyone's guiding theory of the good is worthy of having space to develop, even if all beliefs are not equal. But when you begin from the assumption that only your beliefs are true, it's not too hard to see how you would need to redefine tolerance is an unnatural way just to sleep with your conscience at night.

Take another example of this effort to redefine natural concepts. When we think of the word "happiness," we're met with a complex set of ideas. Synonyms come to mind: pleasure, joy, peace, satisfaction, contentment, excitement, and so forth. Happiness is one of those broad concepts that contains multitudes. If you ask the average person whether happiness is something to be valued and sought, most people would likely agree that it is. But if you ask those same people how one is to achieve happiness, the range of answers will be very broad and may even be contradictory.

This is probably because happiness is such an intensely personal topic. If what we mean, at a base level, is that happiness is to have my preferences realized in a given moment, then happiness can move and shift among people and within a person's own life. For instance, I prefer to have enough resources so that I can satisfy all of my needs while at the same time having enough left over so that I can enjoy leisure time, my relationships, and my self-actualization projects. But quantifying this need at a given time period is very difficult to do. For that reason, I am working hard to sacrifice some of my time now so that later in life I will have enough to retire and to spend the remaining years of my life doing what I wish. Another person might decide that waiting for that moment is too much of a risk; life is happening now, so why waste it? For that reason, many people make the decision to spend their surplus today when they can still enjoy it. In many ways, this comes down to a matter of individual preference.

But zealot religions like Mormonism wish to redefine happiness away from this personal quality and to give it a fixed meaning. In Mormonism, I learned and taught that there really is only one form of happiness: to please Heavenly Father. True, there were plenty of things along the way that would bring joy: family, a good profession, hobbies, and so forth; Mormons do not devalue any of those things. But all of those things are either done in the service of Heavenly Father or they are products of that service, blessings that he bestows on the righteous. Plenty of religious beliefs include pleasing a deity as an element of happiness; zealot faiths are not unique on that front. But zealot faiths direct the adherent to focus *solely* on serving their god and claim that *only* they have the clearest path to happiness. Because Mormonism teaches that only Mormon doctrine can give someone full access to god, only Mormonism will truly make you happy. Speaking of those who have left Mormonism, the current president of the Mormon church, Russell Nelson, recently said that in his almost 100 years of life, he has "never met anyone who was happier because he or she violated covenants made with God."[38] For zealots, no matter how happy you think you are, you're never going to be as happy as they are.

What's also ironic about this redefining of happiness is that it is often paired with so much of what we would consider suffering. For example, I was told that there was never going to be a time in my life as a Mormon that would quite compare to missionary service. Other than parenthood, missionary service ranks as one of the highest duties a man can perform in the Mormon church. I was told that the amount of happiness it would bring me would make whatever the world could offer me pale in comparison. Yet, nothing about that experience would come close to the standard definition of happiness: I lived dirt poor, paid the Mormon church for the right to do it, dealt with harassment and rejection on an hourly basis, suffered through relationships with antisocial companions, and worked 24 hours a day, 7 days a week for the Mormon church. Ask me at the time if I had been happy, and I would have told you, "Of course I am! Heavenly Father is pleased

---

[38] Walker, Sydney. "President Nelson: 'We will build temples. You will build people prepared to enter them.'" *Deseret News* (Nov. 13, 2022).

with me!" Ask me now? All I can see is a 20-year-old boy who was stressed out of his mind. It is this suffering/happiness connection that zealotry depends upon; the more one encounters suffering, the more one is pleasing god, and the more one is happy. Recently, an apostle for the Mormon church, Jeffrey Holland, said: "To be a follower of Jesus Christ, one must sometimes carry a burden – your own or someone else's – and go where sacrifice is required and suffering is inevitable."[39] You have to admire the "I win/you lose" nature of that thinking: if life is good, it's happiness, and if life is bad, it's also happiness – provided it's all in the service of deity. There's no defeating that sort of thinking.

Perhaps the worst example of the definition problem, though, is one that is as loathsome as it is foundational to the zealot attitude. The concept of "love," like happiness and tolerance, is one that is inherently part of the human condition. Like justice, we generally know what love is when we see it, even if we can't articulate a clear definition of it. I have had many relationships in my life that I believe were grounded in some form of love. I have been married to the same woman for 16 years, a marriage that has survived many changes because it has been rooted in love. I have family members who, no matter how far we have drifted apart, are still people I love greatly. All of these relationships share similar patterns: I want to be around these people, I am willing to

---

[39] Holland, Jeffrey R. "Lifted Up upon the Cross," *Semiannual General Conference* (October 2022). Holland goes on to list examples of suffering, including those "who I know many who wrestle with wrenching matters of identity, gender, and sexuality." So at least part of what he means by suffering is "following Mormon teachings against all odds."

sacrifice time/energy/resources for them, I share the same interests as them, and I feel confident that they feel similarly about me.

But there is one relationship that has taught me way more about love than any other I have ever had: parenthood. Although parenthood is a lifelong learning process, I started to realize on Day 1 of being a father that the love I felt for this tiny creature was much deeper and much more profound than any I had ever felt. It has been a mixture of many things. It is my son's innocence and vulnerability; I know that without me, my child would not be able to survive and flourish. It is my son's eagerness and curiosity for everything; seeing the world through a child's eyes makes you realize all the little wonders that you had taken for granted for so long. It is my son's future; I know that the routes his life will follow can and will be many, and that he needs all the resources he can get now to choose the path that best fits him. Above all, it's the fact that *he* seems to love *me*: completely and unwaveringly. Yes, there are difficult moments; I was well into my 30s when I had a child, and my life has been completely upended by this small, pint-sized force. There are days when I wonder if anything I am doing is working. But I have never yet seen the love my child has for me diminish in his eyes.

You who are parents, ask yourself what it means to be a good parent. There are probably a hundred things any one of us could come up with at a given time, knowing full well we aren't doing even half of them at once. There is no one, tried and true way to be a good parent, as each child is unique and requires individualized care. But I think our intuitions tell us when we see something that raises red flags in parenting; even if we don't know what makes a good parent, we can hazard a guess as to what makes a *not good* parent. Parents who abuse their children – physically, emotionally, sexually – are probably not doing a very good job following the parenting manual. Parents who neglect their children or abandon them for selfish reasons are also suspect. Moreover, parents who have the power to intervene and prevent harm from coming to their children and don't do so are also not what we would consider to be good parents. What is common to all of these situations is a child who was brought into existence by a person, who depends greatly on that person and naturally trusts them implicitly, and who has now had that relationship of trust violated – perhaps irreparably.

The love that is at the center of this relationship is unconditional. It has no qualifiers attached to it. I have friends who I love very much, but I can imagine scenarios – however remote they are – where they could do things that would diminish my love for them. The same could be true of family members and partners. But when it comes to my child, it's very difficult for me to imagine something he could do to diminish my love for him. I think there is something natural in us that says that we all need at least one place in this world where no matter how hard it gets and no matter how rejected we are, we still have one place where we can find peace. I think we call that place "home." It's that motivating ideal that gives parents a standard to follow as they parent. Do we do it perfectly? No, but good parents are those who keep trying to make home for their child.

Zealot faiths like Mormonism corrupt this natural definition of love. For such faiths, love is always conditional; it always comes with caveats, footnotes, and qualifiers. This is because rather than start with this most basic form of love – the natural one between a parent and child – zealot faiths start with an idealized, hypothetical love grounded in their religious beliefs. Take Mormonism, for instance. Mormonism preaches love to anyone who will listen. Love one another, show love at home, love thy neighbor as thyself, Heavenly Father is a god of love are all common Mormon phrases. A key facet of the Mormon plan of salvation is that families, if they are sealed together through Mormon ordinances and a temple marriage and the members prove worthy, can be eternal. Where other faiths marry people "until death do us part," Mormons marry beyond the grave. Mormonism, then, looks to be a religion that has love as one of its features.

But let's be clear what Mormonism means by love. Love is an expression that Heavenly Father shows to his children. True love – defensible, actual, ideal, and perfect – is love that Heavenly Father shows. Mormonism teaches that we should pattern our earthly love after this heavenly version of it. So, the task for the would-be loving Mormon is to figure out how Heavenly Father defines love. In this case, Heavenly Father's love looks drastically different from the natural definition I've described above. On the one hand, Heavenly Father occasionally gives blessings to the righteous as a reward for their loyalty; on the other hand, he could just as easily *not* give those blessings, too. There are examples in Mormon history of people being healed by faith and Mormon priesthood power – an expression of love from a divine parent. But there are also examples of similarly situated people who *didn't* get such blessings, despite their apparent worthiness. Sometimes

Heavenly Father saves his prophets, martyrs, and missionaries, while at other times he doesn't. The ways of the Lord are mysterious indeed.

Moreover, the Mormon doctrine of the plan of salvation shows just how Heavenly Father feels toward his children. In the premortal existence, a third of his children that he brought into existence were cast out when they refused to participate in his simulation. By the time the world has ended, another very small portion of the human race will be destroyed in Outer Darkness with the other rebellious children and another very large portion will be sent to live away from Heavenly Father. That second group will have a nice spot to live, certainly, but they will forever be Heavenly Father's servants, receiving instructions indirectly from him through Jesus and his chosen few, and they will never, ever get to be in his presence again – they can't come home. Only those who do everything he commands will earn that reward – a reward that includes the right to continue this cycle of creation, testing, and sorting of other human spirits for eternity. At the center of this plan is Jesus Christ, god's beloved son, the one that is the carbon copy of him. Despite being spotless and without sin, this plan that won't even redeem majority of god's children hinges on the fact that Heavenly Father has him brutally tortured and killed at some point in history. In Mormonism, the crucifixion is only one part of that torture; the moment in the Garden of Gethsemane, in which Jesus bleeds from every pore, is the true sacrificial event. There Heavenly Father places on Jesus every human sin, suffering, and pain – for *each* individual person *as if* Jesus were that person – as recompense. And for what? For all the ways Heavenly Father's children disobey him.

Mormonism has slowly begun to say the quiet part out loud on this front. Within my own lifetime, the word "love" has become used less and less in conjunction with "unconditional" when describing Heavenly Father's love. For example, current Mormon church president, Russell Nelson, gave an entire talk about the unconditionality of Heavenly Father's love.[40] Heavenly Father might *care* about you, in the sense that he wants you to be happy. But love? No, that's something reserved for those who follow him, for those who emulate him, and for those who live so much like him that they become carbon copies of him. As another Mormon apostle, Dallin Oaks, has said, "Some seem to value God's love because of their hope that His love is so great and so unconditional that it will mercifully excuse them from obeying His laws. In contrast, those who understand God's plan for His children know that God's laws are invariable, which is another great evidence of His love for His children."[41] In other words, Heavenly Father loves some people more than others. And if you would like more of his love, all you have to do is exactly what he says; the more you do, the more you will be like him, and the more he'll love you. You can find similar patterns of thought in other zealot Christian faiths.

There are at least two things that should be shocking about this redefinition. The first is that it is such a superficial cover up

---

[40] Nelson, Russell M. "Divine Love," *Ensign* (Feb. 2003).
[41] Oaks, Dallin H. "Love and Law," *Semiannual General Conference* (Oct. 2009).

for social and political beliefs. For example, at exactly the same time the Mormon church has begun to redefine love, it has used its outsized monetary and political power to push back on political events that would give others the right to live in whatever way they choose. In the area of LGBTQ rights, the Mormon church has a long history of opposition and is still actively working to end the recognition of things like gay marriage. If your starting point is that "God loves some of us more than others," then it's not too much of a logical leap to conclude that you can use whatever power you have to "correct" what you don't like in others. The Mormon church cannot abide a world in which the "wicked" get to do as they wish without their say so, but they can couch it as "love" for others to want to correct them. Pick other Mormon church policies – a priesthood ban for women, some forms of contraception, cohabitation, and so forth – and it's not too hard to draw a line from this conditional "love" to those features.

The second, and more troubling lesson when it comes to the zealot redefinition of love, is how much license it gives individual adherents to abuse others. Mormonism teaches that God is perfect. If his form of conditional "love" is perfect, then shouldn't I also emulate that love? Shouldn't *my* love also be conditional? If my home is my own heaven and my children are my own creation, then shouldn't I treat them the same way god does? If I set rules, shouldn't I love the ones who follow those rules and show less love to the ones who don't? This is precisely the line of thought that many Mormons have taken. For example, that same Dallin Oaks and another Mormon leader, gave a pre-cleared "interview" with a member of the Mormon church's media department about gay marriage. In that interview, they were asked what a good Mormon parent should do if their child were to come out as gay, were living with their partner, and were wanting to come home, say for a visit or for the holidays. Here's the answer:

> *ELDER OAKS: That's a decision that needs to be made individually by the person responsible, calling upon the Lord for inspiration. I can imagine that in most circumstances the parents would say, 'Please don't do that. Don't put us into that position.' Surely if there are children in the home who would be influenced by this example, the answer would likely be that. There would also be other factors that would make that the likely answer.*
>
> *I can also imagine some circumstances in which it might be possible to say, 'Yes, come, but don't expect to stay overnight. Don't expect to be a lengthy house guest. Don't expect us to take you out and introduce you to our friends, or to deal with you in a public situation that would imply our approval of your "partnership."*
>
> *There are so many different circumstances, it's impossible to give one answer that fits all.*
>
> *ELDER WICKMAN: It's hard to imagine a more difficult circumstance for a parent to face than that one. It is a case-by-case determination. The only thing that I would add to what Elder Oaks has just said is that I think it's important as a parent to avoid a potential trap arising out of one's anguish over this situation.*

> *I refer to a shift from defending the Lord's way to defending the errant child's lifestyle, both with him and with others. It really is true the Lord's way is to love the sinner while condemning the sin. That is to say we continue to open our homes and our hearts and our arms to our children, but that need not be with approval of their lifestyle. Neither does it mean we need to be constantly telling them that their lifestyle is inappropriate. An even bigger error is now to become defensive of the child, because that neither helps the child nor helps the parent. That course of action, which experience teaches, is almost certainly to lead both away from the Lord's way.*

Note where the love really is here. Between the Mormon church's teachings and the child, the teachings get priority, since following those as a parent will give *you* greater access to Heavenly Father's love. The god at the heart of Mormonism says, "It's either that kid or me. If you pick them, fine. But you can't ever come home." That trickle-down parental abuse is what many Mormon families adopt when their children separate from the church. Having watched this firsthand, there is literally *nothing* off the table for a Mormon parent when they find out that their child is drifting away from the church; some of the most awful words and deeds have been done by well-meaning Mormon parents who are trying to show "divine love" to their children. Even when you, the child, have embraced the reality that the relationship is over, the "parental love" just keeps coming, in much the same way that you can never escape god's conditional "love."

It's small wonder why zealot faiths go down this path. At least in the Abrahamic tradition, they have a ready example of the kind of love Heavenly Father expects. I have cited Abraham's sacrifice of Isaac multiple times in this book, but here is where the knife meets the flesh, as it were. What this redefinition of love asks any would-be adherent to do is be willing to sacrifice even the thing we love the most in the name of a god we can't see, who hides himself as much as possible, and who places overwhelming demands upon us followed by threats. The god of Abraham might have spared Isaac. But that same god has broken families, ostracized children, produced many sleepless, weeping nights, and all because he demands – nay, commands – our love. Lest you think only Mormons behave this way, look around at every Christian, Muslim, and Jewish sect for echoes of this barbaric, cruel, and insane view of human life. For a god that sees us as his creation first and his servants second, there is no room for diversity or disagreement. It's his "love" or it's nothing.

I could cite other examples of the ways in which zealot faiths redefine uncontroversial concepts that are so inherent to the human condition, but what they all boil down to is this: whatever we think is real, is not real in the eyes of a zealot. If I were to point out to the average Mormon how unnatural all of those definitions are, they would shrug and say, "Yes, that's the point." Whatever nature has made me think tolerance, happiness, and love are, they are products of my sinful nature. No matter how much good those concepts can do in the world, they're not enough. As I've said before, the Mormon equivalent of "original sin" is the "natural man," who is "an enemy to god." Well, whatever that natural man thinks is right is almost certainly an affront to Heavenly Father. Can Heavenly Father tolerate a natural, sinful human being in his presence? Is the point of the plan of salvation and its simulation to bring children back home under natural conditions? Not at all. No, what that natural man needs is a good stiff dose of redefinition. Here, these are the right definitions of tolerance, happiness, and love. Use these and Heavenly Father will be satisfied. Sure, you'll suffer in the process, but in the long run, you'll be better off. We promise.

I often asked myself why I was so caught up on the particularities of the Mormon plan of salvation. When so many others left Mormonism because of its origins, its history, and its policies, why was I OK with all of those but hung up on this doctrinal point? I think it boiled down to a very simple inconsistency between Mormon divine love and my intuitions. I had two loving parents in my life, who, despite not being perfect on some cosmic scale, gave my siblings and me a very good life. Parenting is challenging, but there was no question in my mind that either of my parents would do literally anything in the world for me if necessary. Never did I feel like I was some object in my parents' lives, but a cherished, loved child. I was lucky to have parents who didn't just love me for what I *did* but for *who* I was. Meanwhile, I had been told and had taught others that Heavenly Father was the supreme embodiment of love. But there was a lurking incongruence between the love I had felt in my home and the kind of love Heavenly Father said was the root of his plan. In my home, I always felt I could come back and be accepted. But with Heavenly Father, I was never sure; I was constantly begging, pleading, repenting, working, checking, praying, fasting, obeying, sacrificing, consecrating so that he would let me back in the front door. Something felt off about that.

While I did not recognize it at the time, what finally broke me with zealotry was this definitional problem. On the belief spectrum, my knowledge had already begun to slacken, and I was less committed to many of the doctrines of the Mormon church. But even in that two-year period of introspection, the old zealot in me hadn't given up; the attitude spectrum was still very much one-sided. I had so many concepts defined for me for so long that I was now scrambling for my own definitions, even if my beliefs were shifting. It took having a child myself – to stand in the capacity of the *parent* this time – to see it. What if there came a time when my son came out as gay? What if he chose not to be Mormon? What if he went down a path that Emily and I had not envisioned for him and that deviated from Mormonism in some way? Was I prepared to choose Mormonism over him? Was I prepared to sacrifice my son for some set of rigid beliefs? No, I wasn't. And I didn't think it made me a bad parent for saying so. So, then what right did god have in calling himself "Heavenly Father," when he was so willing to toss away his children on similar grounds? If that was the kind of parent I was going to be with for eternity, I would like to have nothing to do with him.

What separated me from the likes of Matthew Taylor Coleman was this: no voice in my head, no matter how much I believed it, was going to get me to kill my son.

3. The Triumphant Apatheist

As I come to the close of this book, I want to return to the spirit of the first chapter and bring apatheism into focus. Why does all of this matter? Why should anyone care at all whether there are apatheists or zealots in the world? Why should I care whether I am an apatheist or what that label even means? Why do I need to describe these attitudes in this way? Beyond the answers I articulated in the first chapter, I think apatheism matters for quite a few reasons.

First and foremost, an apatheistic attitude is a counterpoint to the authoritarian spirit of zealotry. By calling zealotry authoritarian, I am not doing so to tie it in some way with political ideologies like "nationalism" or "fascism," nor am I trying to suggest that zealots somehow condone dictatorships. What I mean by authoritarian spirit is something more basic than that. Zealotry is an attitude that cannot condone difference and seeks to elevate one set of religious beliefs over all others. At its most extreme, a zealot attitude would like to see the world conform fully and completely to the religious beliefs it espouses. Moreover, zealot faiths often see religious beliefs as hierarchical, with a supreme being in the unquestionable position as leader and his earthly servants ranked in accordance with their allegiance to him. It is part of the zealot mentality to accept one's place in that social order and to ensure – through methods like proselytizing, political action, and cultural acceptance – that others do the same.

I am not suggesting that anything about this mentality is necessarily bad; such value-driven questions are for another day and would require more space than I have available here. But it is enough to say that apatheism serves as a helpful counterpoint to the zealotry's authoritarian spirit. Apatheism, with its indifference and reciprocity, offers a competing attitude to the world without sacrificing underlying beliefs. You can be a Christian, a Muslim, a Jew, or an atheist without requiring that everyone else agree with your beliefs. For the apatheist, diversity of religious beliefs is a reality of the world, and one that will not disappear any time soon. Apatheists respond to zealots by denying the need for molding society into one homogenous group. Nor does an apatheist see themselves as "under attack" if there are others in the world who do not share their beliefs. Because apatheists do not share the same level of intensity to their beliefs that zealots do, apatheists do not have to worry about judging others against one benchmark, but according to a diverse set of principles that includes more than religious beliefs. In this way, I think apatheism serves a "checks and balances" function on zealotry.

Second, apatheism adds nuance to the discussion of religious beliefs. As I mentioned in the first chapter, we spend way too much of our time categorizing people according to belief. When we label someone a "Muslim" or an "Evangelical Christian" or an "atheist," all too often we have a prepackaged set of stereotypes in our minds. We think that beliefs make the person and that, therefore, they must make attitudes as well. It is possibly true that some beliefs are *more likely* to lead to a zealot or apatheistic attitude, but that does not necessarily have to be the case. Unfortunately, though, we often treat them as being identical. Moreover, these mental categories might be helpful with short-term thinking;

being able to quickly assess a person simply by knowing their beliefs is a mental shortcut that saves us a lot of energy. But they are unfair to the individual person and destructive for long-term thinking; they corrupt relationships, destabilize communities, and further isolate us into hostile groups.

What I said in the first chapter should be abundantly clear by now. It is beyond time for us to break out of that one-dimensional thinking. There is more to a person than their beliefs. When it comes to religious beliefs, a person also possesses attitudes toward those beliefs. As I have argued in this book, it is actually the attitudes that we are often so worked up about. But rather than meet that fact head on, we try to pigeonhole that discussion into beliefs. By doing so, we unnecessarily stigmatize people who have religious beliefs but who do not share the attitudes of their fellow believers. For example, the Mormon *church* may adopt an awful lot of zealot policies. And there are quite a few zealot Mormons in the world. But I have met thousands of Mormons in my lifetime and continue to have good relationships with many of them. Not all Mormons are zealots. There are many Mormons who deeply and passionately believe their religion just as much as their zealot peers. But unlike those peers, they are not very concerned with a world that isn't Mormon. They don't see every event in the world as an attack on Mormonism and, while they would be happy to see friends and family join the Mormon church, they also aren't going to let that stand in the way of such relationships. They are also actively working to change the culture of Mormonism to make it more accepting of diverse lifestyles and personalities. Lumping in these individuals with their more zealot peers simply because they believe similar religious claims is not only unfair but illogical. This same phenomenon is true of nearly every other religious or irreligious group in the nation. When we recognize that apatheism and zealotry add an additional layer of discussion to religion beyond mere belief, we can change our collective discourse to one that is more nuanced and respecting of individuals.

Third, in a similar vein, I think that apatheism specifically can be empowering to individuals who normally feel that they do not have a voice or who are often pressured by the vocal zealots in their religious communities. When we name something, we give it power and legitimacy. Far too often, religious people who do not adhere to every dogma, doctrine, and declaration of a faith are treated as second class citizens by their believing peers. They are labelled as "lukewarm" members of their community. In an example that I have consciously ignored until now, Kyle Beshears, a Southern Baptist pastor who has written a thing or two about Mormonism, penned *Apatheism: How We Share When They Don't Care*, in which he does a significant amount of hand wringing over apatheism. He sees it as a problem to be rooted out, that indifference to belief is a threat to be neutralized. From my own experience, I saw firsthand the kind of marginalization that occurs in the Mormon church against those who are "not Mormon enough." "Jack" Mormons and "inactive" Mormons are at the fringe of the community and are just as ripe for saving as the non-Mormon world. To the Mormon church, there is only one path to salvation, and it is walking up to every covenant that the

Mormon church requires of its faithful. There is no middle lane on the straight and narrow path to heaven.

But to those who are in the lukewarm category and who have been called problematic, broken, rebellious, or confused, I have this to say: stop listening. Your religious or irreligious beliefs are not defined by the zealots that happen to control your community or have control of the microphone at the moment. Religious organizations in the United States and in many parts of the West make tremendous amounts of tax-free money by convincing people that it is their way or the highway. The threat of ostracization or damnation is all too often tied to power and money. What you are told is that you apparently don't believe hard enough or that you don't believe in the right way or that you must not understand what you believe. Apatheism invites you to boldly respond that, yes, as a matter of fact you do believe and you're very comfortable with where you've arrived with those beliefs, thanks very much. Confidently declaring to the world that you are an apatheist, whether a theistic apatheist or an atheistic apatheist, lets the zealots in the world know that you are not going to kowtow to some magisterial elite that thinks there is only one way to live. You, and only you, are in the best position to know just how much energy you are able to give your religious or irreligious beliefs.

Finally, these previous points raise the most personal takeaway from apatheism, which is that it allows people to keep their beliefs without sacrificing something in the offing. We are now well into the 21st Century and the range of things that require our attention is daunting. In many ways, our technologically advanced world has improved our lives: greater and more immediate access to information, greater availability of goods and services, greater mobility, both physically and socioeconomically, and great longevity – at least if you are born in the West. But with those improvements have come costs to our mental health, our relationships, our time, and our capacity to develop as human beings. Whereas a human being 6000 years ago might have faced one or two catastrophic events that caused them anxiety in their lifetime, the 21st Century human hears about a new catastrophic event before every meal. We are hardwired to respond to threats, and the constant barrage of emergencies – whether some asinine event on social media or the rumblings of World War III – is exhausting our ability to function.

Is it too much to ask that we cut ourselves a break in the area of religious belief? An apatheist doesn't think so. Apatheism tells us that it's more than OK to dial down the volume on the internal religious speaker. Apatheism allows religious beliefs to cook on a gentle simmer, rather than get the attention of a filet mignon in Hell's Kitchen. Apatheism is an attitude that lets us prioritize the immediate in a given day and confidently leave the cosmic for another. Some people might thrive under conditions of zealotry; if so, to each their own. But not every believer or non-believer will. Apatheism creates a space for such individuals to be themselves without sacrificing everything else in a chaotic and confusing world.

What if we give it a shot?

Moving On

In three words I can sum up everything I've learned about life: it goes on.
— Robert Frost

As I close out this book, I want to recap where we have been and what yet remains to be done. I set about in this book to make the following claim: that apatheism is a consistent, articulable attitude directed toward religious beliefs. My goal was to show what apatheism is and what it isn't. To do so, I first explained the difference between beliefs and attitudes, how they relate to another, and the way they work independently. I then went on to define apatheism's opposite, zealotry. In defining these two concepts, I explained that zealotry has two major features: intensity toward beliefs and exceptionalism with regard to those beliefs. Apatheism reverses these two features and embraces indifference or passivity toward beliefs and reciprocity toward to others' beliefs. I have also described the three major religious beliefs to which apatheism can be directed: a belief in a deity, a belief in the deity's interaction with the known universe, and a belief in loyalty to that deity. In so doing, I showed how apatheism can be woven into both private and public contexts. All of this builds to reinforce my major description of apatheism: *Apatheism is the philosophical attitude of indifference and reciprocity, both public and private, to (1) the question of the existence of a deity, (2) the interaction of that deity with the universe, and/or (3) the value of loyalty to that deity.*

I want to stress a few points that I raised at the beginning of the book and to forecast other questions that need to be addressed in the discussion of apatheism. My sole goal in this book was to lay the groundwork for a conversation around apatheism. I continue to believe that it has not been given the attention that it deserves. Many individuals don't even know this concept exists, and those who do dismiss it as "lazy religious thinking." This book is intended to change both of those reactions. I hope that this discussion has shown that apatheism is not in any way lazy thinking, but a legitimate philosophical attitude that one can proudly declare as his or her own. Moreover, I believe that, as more people come to embrace apatheism as the label for a phenomenon that already exists, its legitimacy will continue to increase. The apatheists are already out there; this book is simply a tool to describe what attitudes they have and how they relate to their religious beliefs. So, I am confident that this book, while only a sketch, will generate a much-needed conversation about religious commitments, especially in the United States.

That said, I recognize that a lot remains to be discussed. I can think of at least two questions that are a high priority after laying the groundwork in this short book. The first is the normative question that follows from apatheism: *should* a person be an apatheist instead of a zealot? I have taken as many pains as I can to withhold judgment on a person's choice to be a zealot. The examples of zealotry that I have included in the book are extreme and selected for that purpose; I have wanted to show what zealotry looks like when taken to its logical conclusion. I have done so *only* to show what apatheism is. But remember that these attitudes are a spectrum, and, therefore, one can be a zealot by degrees or a zealot about some beliefs but not others. There is nothing in this book that should suggest zealotry on its face is bad. For that reason, I reiterate what I said in the preface: that a person should withhold judgment on both apatheism and zealotry until we can establish what those concepts are.

But now that we have a grip on what we mean by these attitudes in the religious belief context, the "should" question deserves its day. Cards on the table: I do believe that more people should be apatheists. I do strongly believe that the world would be better with fewer – maybe even no – religious zealots. When it comes to an individual's religious beliefs, I tend to not get too worked up. Unlike hard atheists, I am not taking the position here that the world should be purged of religious *beliefs*. Maybe it should, maybe it should not. That conversation has had a lot of ink and blood spilled in it, and far be it for me to add more. But I do believe that when it comes to *attitudes* about religious beliefs, we would all be better off in a world of apatheists. I believe that apatheism is fertile soil for a person to pursue their own life choices and to express their autonomy. I believe that apatheism makes for better individuals, families, and communities. And I believe that a state that adopts apatheism as its principle of religious freedom is a much more just state than one that either ignores religious attitudes altogether or creates a breeding ground for zealotry. I believe that the United States has historically slid between the two and that we are entering an era of the latter. I believe that is political and cultural suicide.

For that reason, my next project is to turn to the "should" question. I hope, in the near future, to produce a book that argues forcefully for apatheism and encourages apatheists to spread their attitude to other communities in positive ways. In so doing, I hope to address the fear on the religious believer's part that apatheism is just a roundabout way to destroy religion, while addressing the atheist's concern that apatheism gives cover to irrational, wishful thinking. I'm hopeful that between now and then there will be plenty of time to include other voices in that conversation. It would be a dream come true for others to participate in "apatheistic studies" to expand the sketch that I have made in this book.

The second immediate question I see is more practical: *how* should one be an apatheist or *how* is apatheism possible in the real world? As someone who is both a political theorist and a constitutional law scholar, I believe that theory should have an impact on practice. The application of a theory to problems and the identification of solutions is often referred to as "praxis," in which we develop principles of action. Since I have developed in this book a theory of apatheism, it will definitely be necessary to transition to praxis, identifying the ways an apatheist acts toward themself, their fellow persons, their communities, and their states. What is needed is a guide to apatheism.

So, again, for that reason, a subsequent project I intend to take up is just such a guide. In that guide, I hope to describe how to structure one's ethical thinking in the religious context around apatheism. What should an apatheist do when they encounter a coworker who is a zealot or someone who has never thought about these topics? How should an apatheist treat their romantic partner, their family, or their children, especially if some or all of them do not share apatheistic attitudes? Additionally, I think this guide will need to address how an apatheist citizen should behave. What duties is an apatheist under as a voter? How should an apatheist behave in civic discourse? In this guide, I plan to solicit contributions and ideas from others who have adopted an apatheist attitude. In doing so, I believe the guide will better speak for and to the apatheist community.

My hope is that from all of this effort, in a few years' time, we will be having a much more nuanced conversation around religious beliefs.

***

Before I close, I want to end on a personal note about my own apatheist journey. This book has been many years in the making. Although the real heavy lifting has taken a little over a year, it's ultimately born out of almost 40 years of life experiences and my journey away from zealot Mormonism. Trying to write a book about anything *and* root it in one's own experience is a daunting task, one that feels like trying to sweep the sand off a beach while the waves just keep throwing it back. So, I have had to necessarily be judicious in where I focus my attention from my own story for this short volume; otherwise, it would never get off the ground.

But let me offer a few, recent developments relevant to my own story.

The first is that some things just never change, and you need no further proof of that then the endless contact I still get from the Mormon church. Even now, years after the fact and with my position very clearly articulated, I still have to fend off "loving fellowship" from Mormon zealots. Just since the bulk of this project got underway, I can count no less than nine instances of rescue missions conducted by friends and family to reel my wife and me back into the fold. For example, as I was working on revisions for this book one afternoon, I got a message on a social media app, out of the blue, from a Mormon missionary who apparently works in my area. I have had no prior contact with this woman, have no mutual connection with her, and have no reason whatsoever to be talking with her. Yet, none of that dissuaded her from connecting with me and nonchalantly asking about me. I figured I would play along and asked how she knew me/where this contact was coming from, like any normal person would when a stranger interacts with them. Almost immediately, she gave me the pitch: "I'm a missionary for the Church of Jesus Christ of Latter-day Saints! I just add people on [social media app] to share the gospel with others to see if they are interested in learning more!" Needless to say, I respectfully but firmly explained that I was not going to be a good use of her time. There have been other instances of well-meaning (and sometimes not well-meaning) outreach by Mormons. All I see in these is yet further evidence of zealot exceptionalism: no matter how often you ask for space and the freedom to be you, they never really think you mean it. Their attitude toward beliefs that they are certain justifies them in using whatever means necessary to make their religious dreams a reality. I expect that cycle will repeat itself for a long time.

The second is that some things occasionally do change. As I am about to send off this draft to my publisher, the Mormon church has been charged by the U.S. Securities and Exchange Commission for failing to disclose its stake in a $100 billion investment fund called Ensign Peak.[42] The church settled these charges quickly and without much commentary; the fund will pay the SEC a $4 million penalty and the church itself will pay $1 million. The settlement and the haste are not at all shocking. The last thing the Mormon church wants is public examination of its financial dealings by the U.S. government; it is already having to weather a similar storm of examination by the Australian government.[43] The Mormon church recognizes that the Establishment and Free Exercise clauses in the U.S. Constitution shield it significantly from scrutiny, but there is only so much a political community can turn a blind eye to before enough is enough. I hope that time is coming for the sake of all those individual Mormons who have been told by zealots their whole lives to make paying tithes to the Mormon church the "first priority of all [their] other financial obligations."[44] There have been many recent shows,

---

[42] "SEC Charges The Church of Jesus Christ of Latter-day Saints and Its Investment Management Company for Disclosure Failures and Misstated Filings." Press Release, U.S. Securities and Exchange Commission (Feb. 21, 2023).

[43] "Mormon church accused of ripping of taxpayers by millions of dollars," 60 Minutes Australia (Oct. 30, 2022).

[44] Johnson, Daniel L. "The Law of Tithing," *Semiannual General Conference* (October 2006). See also "Paying Tithing First Actually Helps Your Budget," *LDS Self-Reliance Services* (July 27, 2018).

books, and podcasts about Mormonism. While there are a few good documentaries about Mormon off-shoot groups, there has yet to be a definitive, thoughtful, and factually unbiased assessment of Mormonism – one that no Mormon can claim is inaccurate or "anti-Mormon," but which gives an account of Mormonism outside the church's P.R.-friendly lens. Things like this SEC settlement and the Australian investigation show this is long overdue.

As I said in the preface, I am now a happy apatheist. My religious beliefs are complex, a mix of local atheism, strong agnosticism, and wishful thoughts about things like the afterlife and the soul. I have reached a stage in my life where those wishful questions do not trouble me much, even if I find them metaphysically interesting. But I am learning that growth is not a destination but a lifetime journey; if the first 30 years of my life taught me anything, it is that a person should give themselves the grace to follow that journey. Moreover, I remain friends with many individuals who have strong religious convictions, some of whom are longtime Mormon friends. We have reached a place of reciprocity: they have their beliefs, I have mine, and we both deprioritize religious beliefs as a factor in our friendships. As someone who is a passionate advocate for societal changes, I constantly overstep my bounds. But I am working diligently to be the kind of apatheist I wish to see in others. Above all, I remain committed to one very important thing: rearing my son in a way that respects his autonomy and allows him to grow into the person he chooses to be.

For that, I think I'm doing a little better than Matthew Taylor Coleman or Abraham.

Acknowledgements

*I think of myself as someone who is filled with love...
whose only purpose in life is to achieve love.*
- Stephen Fry

I've learned that there is nothing a person can't do without help, and that is no less true in the case of this book. It would be a massive failure on my part not to thank the many people who have made this book and the related projects possible. First and foremost, I want to thank the team at *Hypatia Press* and *Ockham Publishing*, including Rob Johnson and David G. McAfee, my commissioning editors. They have been enormously helpful, patient, and thoughtful throughout this process.

The research that went into this first book has mostly been my own (and my fault, if there are errors), but I have had a support team that I could not have done without. A few students at University of Wisconsin-Eau Claire – Hannah Hawthorne, Grace Justice, Elizabeth TenBarge, and Alex Zanotti – volunteered their time to help research instances of religious violence. Although only a few examples made it into this volume, their work will prove to be invaluable as I take up the next book. In a similar vein, my longtime graduate school friends and methodological geniuses, Dave Bracken and Joe Broad, were an excellent sounding board for defining apatheism and identifying measurement tools that we will use in the next project. Without them (and their constant distraction to play Dungeons & Dragons), I would be up a creek. Finally, in terms of research, I appreciate the comments I got for portions of this book from a panel at *Midwestern Political Science Association*, especially from Gideon Elford, Eduardo Schmidt Passos, and Gent Carrabregu.

On a more personal note, I have to acknowledge my immediate family, who have not only weighed in on this book but on my transition away from Mormonism. My father and mother, Scott and Shauna, and my brother, Alex, have always been a support and stable foundation in my life; my parents taught me early on that learning is the highest goal we can pursue, and I am ever grateful for that commitment. My sister, Ali Kunz Zhanje, and her husband, Ronnie, have been curious and careful contributors to this project – Ali, in terms of my path away from zealotry, and Ronnie, in terms of my development of apatheism. These are my people and always will be, no matter how much we all change and grow.

Finally, I want to thank my wife, Emily. As I have related my story and used it as a focal point for apatheism, you'll notice that she has been a silent main character. Emily perhaps more than any other person displays what I mean by apatheism: preoccupied with other things besides religious beliefs and indifferent to the beliefs of others, while remaining fiercely loyal to the people she cares about. There were a few times in our journey as a couple leaving Mormonism when we thought it was over for us. Those were dark days that I am grateful are in our rearview mirror. We have weathered many storms together and have built a life that we unabashedly live without fear of judgment from others.

Without Emily's constant love, willingness to listen, and thoughtful criticism, I would not have been able to complete this book. This is as much her story as it is mine.

Born and raised in rural southeastern Idaho in a town founded by his Mormon ancestors, Adam Kunz spent the first 25 years of his life living in the heart of "Mormondom." After a life of deep, zealous commitment to Mormonism, he left his small hometown for law school in Washington, D.C., and was airdropped into a world starkly different from the one in which he had been raised. This prompted a decade-long shift in his perspective on faith, society, and the treatment of others.

Today, Adam is an assistant professor at the University of Wisconsin-Eau Claire, where he teaches political philosophy and constitutional law. He holds a Ph.D. from the University of California, Davis, and a J.D. from The George Washington University Law School. He writes and teaches on tolerance, the limits of freedom of religion, and theories of justice. He lives in Eau Claire, Wisconsin, with his wife, son, and two dogs. When he is not writing or teaching, he's playing Dungeons & Dragons or working on his pollinator habitat.